An Illustrated History of the Church

Created and Produced by Jaca Book

The First Christians
From the beginnings to A.D. 180

The Church Established
A.D. 180–381

The End of the Ancient World
A.D. 381–630

The Formation of Christian Europe
A.D. 600–900

The Middle Ages
A.D. 900–1300

**The Church
in the Age of Humanism**
A.D. 1300–1500

Protestant and Catholic Reform
A.D. 1500–1700

The Church in Revolutionary Times
A.D. 1700–1850

The Church and the Modern Nations
A.D. 1850–1920

The Church Today
A.D. 1920-1981

An outline by chapter can be found on the last two pages of this volume.

The Church Today

An Illustrated History of the Church

From 1920 to 1981

Translated by John Drury

Illustrated by
Sandro Corsi [1-19]
Vittorio Belli [20-38]
Franco Vignazia [39-59]

Winston Press   430 Oak Grove   Minneapolis, Minnesota 55403

Published in Italy under the title
Ai nostri giorni: La chiesa e la sua storia
Copyright © 1981 Editoriale Jaca Book.

**Licensed publisher and distributor
of the English-language edition:**
  Winston Press, Inc.
  430 Oak Grove
  Minneapolis, Minnesota 55403
  United States of America

Agents:
Canada—
  LeDroit/Novalis-Select
  135 Nelson St.
  Ottawa, Ontario
  Canada K1N 7R4

Australia, New Zealand, New Guinea, Fiji Islands—
  Dove Communications, Pty. Ltd.
  Suite 1, 60-64 Railway Road
  Blackburn, Victoria 3130
  Australia

Created and produced by Jaca Book, Milan
Color selection: Mediolanum Color Separations
Printing: Gorenjski tisk, Kranj

History Consultant: The Rev. Marvin R. O'Connell
              Professor of History, University of Notre Dame
Winston Staff: Florence Flugaur, Hermann Weinlick—editorial
              Chris Larson—design

Copyright © 1982, English-language edition,
Jaca Book, Milan, Italy. All rights reserved.
Printed in Yugoslavia.

Library of Congress Catalog Card Number: 78-67840
ISBN: 0-86683-160-6

5 4 3 2 1

An Illustrated History of the Church

The Church Today

Introduction

This last volume in *An Illustrated History of the Church* traces the life of the Christian community from the end of the first World War down to our own day. It is a story filled with shadows long and deep. The twentieth century has proved to be a time of unspeakable horrors which make it difficult indeed for us to accept those theories of human progress so optimistically put forward by our ancestors. Ruthless oppression, concentration camps, terrible economic depressions, the slaughter of millions in political and ethnic purges, the holocaust of European Jews, religious persecution, vast populations condemned to perpetual malnutrition, terrorism, torture, war, and the rumor of war, fought with the most devastating weapons—all these assaults upon human life and dignity are sad reminders of how desperately we and our world stand in need of redemption. Nor can we Christians simply sit back and condemn the hideous and much publicized crimes of Hitler and Stalin and Mao Zedong, since we bear our share of the century's guilt in our racial hatreds, in our greed and wastefulness, in the degradation of the poor among us, in our exploitation of each other, in our indifference to the poor, the naked, and the homeless in lands less favored than ours.

Yet through all this gloom there shine shafts of brilliant light which can lift the heart of the Christian believer. We witness the courage of Dietrich Bonhoeffer, martyred by the Nazis. We go with Mother Teresa on her mission of mercy through the slums of Calcutta. We listen to good Pope John as he urges us to embrace the world so that we can help to sanctify it. We stand in awe at the wonderful faith of the Church of Silence, in Russia and China and so many other dark places where Christ still lives in his people, despite the worst the engines of tyranny can do. We ponder the truths discovered or enriched for us by the patient inquiries of Christian scholars. We cherish the hope that our century may see the beginning of the end of those divisions among us Christians which have wounded us for so long. We cheer the ordinary men and women, in every land and of every social class, who fulfill their baptismal promises in all the small, unglamorous events of their lives.

We who have followed the long history of the Church through this series of books cannot really be surprised at this mixture of light and shadow. It has ever been so. The Christian religion is the religion of the cross, and the mission of the Christian people has been in the words of Apostle Paul, "to make up what is lacking in the sufferings of Christ." This may seem a grim and tragic vocation, and in some ways it is. The failures and frustrations we have experienced as Christians in our own century provide plenty of evidence of that. And yet it is, at the same time, a noble calling, a calling to mediation and healing which gives direction and meaning to our lives as no other calling could. We are the forward edge of a great historical movement, the end of which we cannot see but the marvel of which we do not doubt. We are a pilgrim Church, the fathers of the second Vatican Council said, walking, as Jesus did, humbly yet confidently toward the promised land. It is a joyful pilgrimage, for, to quote Paul again, "we celebrate the death of the Lord until he comes." As, in his own good time, he surely will.

Marvin R. O'Connell

1. Europe after World War I

Revolutionary ideas and actions were a part of the century that began in 1901. Science, literature, and the arts looked at the world in new ways. Psychology, psychoanalysis, and philosophy offered new insights into human life. New inventions changed the atmosphere of city life, travel, and communication. In Europe, an important change of government took place in Russia, where the revolution of 1917 not only ended czarist rule (rule by a king-emperor), but also made Communists for the first time rulers of a nation.

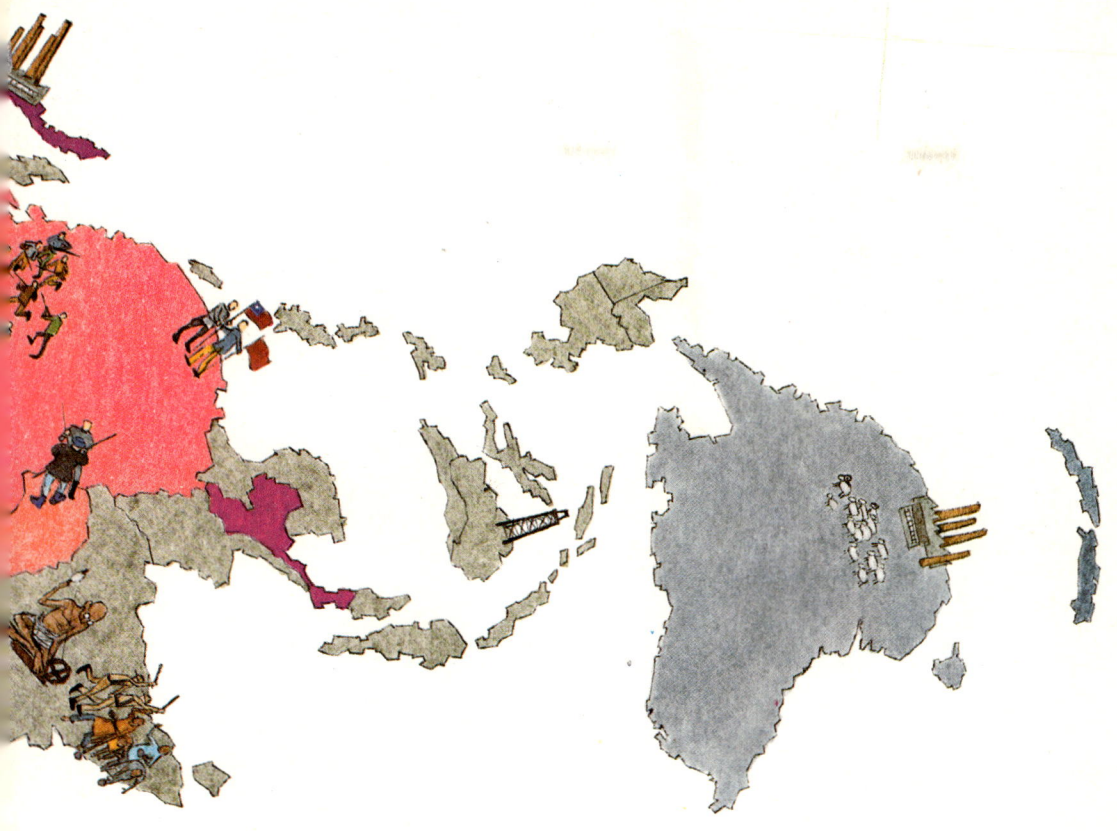

At the end of World War I (1918), ten million men had been killed and about twenty million wounded. Many survivors were disappointed when the more prosperous life they had hoped for did not appear. Many were critical of leaders in government and business. In war they had come to admire the bold military leader who could make fast decisions, strike a blow, get a job done. Other people were weary of war. They might struggle to keep peace at all cost. They might prefer to look the other way when crises that could lead to war appeared.

There were new political arrangements in Europe after the various treaties had been signed and put into effect. The victors imposed harsh conditions on defeated Germany. Efforts had been made to place political boundaries along national lines, but problem areas remained. Austria was now a small republic instead of a huge empire. Hungary was an independent country, but millions of Hungarians now lived within the boundaries of new republics in eastern Europe. Many Germans near the Austrian border were now under Italian rule, and other Germans were now living in the new republic of Czechoslovakia. East Prussia was divided from the rest of Germany by a strip of land which gave the new Polish republic an outlet to the Baltic Sea.

There were a new kingdom of Yugoslavia and many small, weak republics: Czechoslovakia, Poland, Lithuania, Latvia, Estonia, and Finland. Statesmen in large nations such as Germany and Russia might try to control the small countries. Also, France feared that Germany would rise to power again. Great Britain feared French and Russian influence in eastern Europe. Closer to Britain, the new republic of Ireland (Eire) was formed, consisting of twenty-six counties in which Roman Catholics were the vast majority. Six counties in the north were largely Protestant because of three hundred years of Scottish and English immigration. They now became part of the United Kingdom (England, Scotland, and Wales). Tensions in northern Ireland between Catholics and Protestants, and pressures for separation from Britain have continued.

Outside Europe, there were changes too. In the Middle East, France and Britain took over various areas which had once been part of the Ottoman Empire. Syria and Lebanon were under French control. Palestine, Jordan, and Iraq were under British control. Most of Africa was still under the colonial rule of European powers. In Asia, valuable territories were ruled by France, Britain, and Holland. China was now a republic, but it was divided and weakened by internal disputes and warring factions. Japan had increased its strength greatly and was eager to play a dominant role in the Far East. Internal troubles occupied the Soviet Union (Russia). The United States was beginning to exert strong influence in Latin America and the Pacific.

2. Hopeful signs of progress and disturbing signals of danger were seen in various developments after World War I.

Nationalistic feelings had grown stronger during the war years (1914-1918). Each nation's labor, business, government, and other institutions, such as the Christian churches, had worked together. Production goals had been set, supplies had been rationed, women hired for many jobs, and everybody had been expected to do his or her job for the nation. Churches had formed committees to aid the war effort and to send chaplains to the soldiers in the battlefields. All this helped to foster the idea of a nation being a united body, in which each part had its proper role to play.

Nationalism has had many positive accomplishments. In the United States, for example, people of different religions, races, and national backgrounds have worked together as Americans to win two world wars, to send a human being to the moon, to struggle for social justice.

But nationalism has sometimes led to feelings of distrust or superiority toward other nations. Sometimes dictators, such as Hitler, appealed to nationalism to justify their actions and to condemn all disagreement within their borders. Even in democracies, some leaders have tried to limit dissent by calling citizens to support the government, as in America's debate over its role in Vietnam. Sometimes Christians have remembered their ties with their own country but have forgotten their bonds with persons of faith all around the world.

The growth of universal suffrage (the right to vote) was a promising sign for democracy in the twentieth century. Universal suffrage now meant that all men and women of a certain age had the right to vote in elections. New Zealand had recognized women's right to vote as early as 1893. While some individual states had given women the vote earlier, voting rights for women were not recognized in national elections in the United States until 1920. Nevertheless real voting rights in the United States have sometimes fallen far short of the ideal expressed in its constitution. Most black Americans were prevented from voting for

many decades. In the early 1920s, the Ku Klux Klan in the South renewed activities directed especially against Blacks.

The postwar period also saw the rise of new political parties. Between 1920 and 1939, Socialist and Communist parties became important forces in European countries. The Christian churches were slow and timid in confronting the dictatorships imposed by Fascism and Nazism. But the political parties of Christian Democrats would play major roles after World War II in many countries, including Germany, Italy, France, Belgium, Chile, and Venezuela.

3. In the Roman Catholic Church, the Liturgical Movement began to be important in church life. The movement brought renewed awareness of the Church as a living community.

The modern Liturgical Movement in the Roman Catholic Church began in the mid 1800s. (Liturgy refers to the Church's public worship; in the Catholic Church, this worship is the Mass, or Eucharist, and the other sacraments.) In the 1850s, the Abbey of Solesmes, France, brought back the use of Gregorian chant for the Catholic faithful at worship. Gregorian chant had originated in the sixth century. It was beautiful, easy to sing, and many church leaders thought this chant would be a good replacement for the sentimental hymns and opera-like music then often used at Mass. This change in music was supported by Pope Pius X in 1903, in his encyclical (letter) on sacred music.

Maria Laach Abbey in Germany contributed to the Liturgical Movement and Pius Parsch did important work in Austria. An outstanding European in this movement was Romano Guardini, who was born in Italy but lived most of his life in Germany. A famous speaker, he attracted large crowds whenever he spoke. He sometimes took groups of people on long hikes. On one such ramble, the group had to take shelter from the rain in a haybarn. Forgetful of time and unaware of the raging storm outside, the group spent several hours listening entranced as Father Guardini spoke about God, Christ, and the Holy Spirit.

Guardini's book *The Spirit of the Liturgy* became famous in liturgical circles. He saw the liturgy as part of people's broader involvement in the Church, the living community centered around Christ. Guardini is also remembered for his book *The Lord*, a detailed study of the person of Jesus.

In the United States, a national center of the Liturgical Movement was St. John's Abbey, Collegeville, Minnesota, an abbey which traces its foundation to the Benedictine Abbey of Metten, Bavaria. In 1927, Father Virgil Michael of St. John's founded a magazine called *Orate Fratres (Pray, Brethren)*, which was later renamed *Worship*. This was the first major publication devoted to liturgical renewal in the English-speaking world.

Liturgical reformers believed that liturgy was a means, not an end. Like all prayer, the liturgy should lift the minds and hearts of people to God. This action would then help people see themselves as a community, sharing in the same worship. But in reality, it was difficult for worshipers to take part meaningfully in the Mass. Mass and sacrament prayers were said in Latin. At Mass, the priest stood with his back to the people at an altar that was usually rather far removed from the congregation. Catholics attended Mass devoutly and received Communion in great numbers, but there was great emphasis on private prayer at Mass and little understanding of worshiping together as a community. Under these circumstances liturgy had become, to some extent, an end in itself.

The words and actions of Pius X supported liturgical reform. He allowed young children to receive Communion and encouraged adults to receive Communion frequently. He said that Communion was not the reward for good behavior (that is, not an end) but a necessary

food for Christians living on earth (that is, a means).

One result of liturgical reform that affected the lives of many American Catholics between 1929 and 1965 was the extremely widespread use of missals (Mass books) with the prayers of the Mass printed side-by-side in Latin and English. Using the missals, Catholics could take part more fully in Mass. In some parishes, the dialogue Mass became popular. At such a Mass, the congregation—speaking in Latin—responded to the priest's prayers and said the Creed and the Lord's Prayer with him.

Pope Pius XII strongly supported the Liturgical Movement in his encyclical on liturgy *(Mediator Dei)* in 1947. Thus the changes in the Roman Catholic liturgy after Vatican Council II (1962 and after) were not entirely unexpected by Catholics—though the changes were nonetheless startling when they actually took place.

4. In 1922, Pope Pius XI became the head of the Roman Catholic Church. He wanted to open the Church to modern science and knowledge. He also wanted the Church to be present in every phase of human life and history.

Pius XI established an Institute for Christian Archeology and had a new public gallery built for the art treasures of the Vatican. Clearly the new pope was not afraid to make contact with the modern world. He never forgot his pastoral mission. He issued many encyclicals on important topics of the day, including marriage and the social teaching of the Church. He urged the practice of spiritual devotions, including devotions to Mary. He canonized Thèrése of Lisieux (the Little Flower). He readily held formal meetings with the many pilgrims who came to Rome. In 1925, he established the feast of Christ the king. As his own motto said, he wanted to see "the peace of Christ under the reign of Christ." Pius XI took various steps to include bishops from many countries in the college of cardinals, and to establish closer ties with the Eastern Churches. He was a fearless, energetic, and appealing pope who continually stressed the importance of knowing and following Jesus Christ in word and deed.

One of the remarkable features of the Roman Catholic Church in recent history has been the high quality of its popes. Benedict XV, the pope of peace and mission work, was followed by Achille Ratti in 1922. The new pope chose to be named Pius XI.

Born in the diocese of Milan in 1857, Ratti early in his life became noted for his scholarship as a church librarian. He edited many documents relating to the history of the Church in Milan and he became very familiar with the work of Ambrose and Charles Borromeo. The example of those two outstanding bishops of Milan remained in his mind throughout his life. In 1919 he was made a bishop, and he became the papal representative to the new republic of Poland. Two years later he was made archbishop of Milan and a cardinal. The scholar and diplomat became a very industrious pastor of souls in Milan, and in February 1922 he was elected pope.

Pius XI knew various foreign languages and had many contacts in other countries. He was familiar with the science and scholarship of his day, and he did much to establish ties between the Church and modern learning. He was a dedicated priest as well, and he never forgot the care of souls.

The new pope began with a surprise, coming out on the balcony of St. Peter's to bless the crowd. It helped to express his desire to settle the argument between the papacy and the Italian government. It also showed his openness to the city of Rome and to the world.

5. During the 1920s, Catholic and Protestant missionary work in China and Japan grew. The Catholic Church consecrated native bishops and also accepted traditional oriental rites as part of Christian religious practice. Among Asian Christians, Kagawa of Japan was an example of tireless, self-sacrificing work.

From the very beginning of his papacy, Pius XI made clear that his main task was to encourage the preaching of the gospel message throughout the world. It was a duty for the whole Catholic Church, he said, from the pope in Rome to individual Catholics in their local parishes.

Because he was convinced that the Church should be truly universal, he wanted newly formed churches in mission lands to be a real part of their local culture and to be headed by native clergy. He also wanted special attention to be paid to the training of native priests, so that non-European Catholics would not be mere imitations of European Catholics.

In 1926, Pius XI consecrated a native Japanese bishop to head the diocese of Nagasaki. He made it clear that the Church should incorporate local and national customs into its life. This was a change from earlier times, when the Roman Catholic Church had feared that keeping local customs would lessen people's real conversion to Christianity. Chinese and Japanese Catholics were now permitted to take part in some of the traditional practices of their native cultures, such as marriage ceremonies and rituals in remembrance of their ancestors. Similar guidelines were given to the Catholic Church in parts of Africa.

National leaders were also emerging in Protestant mission areas. One of the outstanding Japanese Christians of the period was Toyohiko Kagawa (1888-1960), a convert who attended a Presbyterian college and theological seminary. Kagawa chose to live in the slums and serve the poorest and the neediest. His own eyesight was seriously damaged by a disease which he caught from one of the poor people with whom he shared his lodgings. He preached non-violence and love, and he gradually became convinced that much of the poverty around him was due to the industrial revolution in Japan. He himself became a Christian socialist, engaging in all sorts of work to improve social conditions in Japan. But he was attacked by Communists because he opposed their materialist philosophy. This tireless Japanese evangelist made a deep impression on many Christians around the world.

6. In Africa, movements arose that furthered the independence of African peoples from European powers. Muslim and Christian ideals played a part in these activities.

After various European nations took control of Africa in the nineteenth century, African churches seemed to be very much like European churches in worship, customs, and organization. To many Africans, Christianity seemed more European than Christian. Europeans tended to disregard or even scorn native African traditions and views. The Christian God seemed to many Africans to be the God of the white Europeans, on whom they were politically dependent.

However, many Africans did become Christians. Various native movements during this period sought to adapt Christianity to local circumstances and to relate it to the yearnings and ideals of Africans.

Some movements might be called "messianic" because they centered around one figure as the "anointed" leader and guide to a better Africa. Some educated Africans, trained in missionary schools and influenced by Christian ideals, related the Christian message of redemption to their situation of political bondage. Africans loyal to the religion of Islam were also inspired to seek greater freedom and dignity.

One Messianic movement in Africa during this period was started by Simon Kimbangu (1889-1951), a carpenter and evangelist of the Congo.

Kimbangu was a member of the Bakongo tribal nation. In 1921, at the age of 32, he had a prophetic vision and felt entrusted with a great mission. Kimbangu began to preach in village after village, asserting that a golden age could be expected after the second coming of Jesus Christ. He organized a new church,

and his village of Nkambo came to be regarded as the New Jerusalem. Followers flocked to him. Kimbangu himself did not preach a political message. He claimed to have spiritual powers and the ability to heal the sick. He deeply moved many natives of the Congo region, who no longer had a great empire of their own and who were cruelly exploited by the Belgian rulers of the region.

Political opposition to Belgian rule found some expression among members of Kimbangu's Church, who refused to pay taxes and walked off their jobs. The Belgian authorities feared that Kimbangu's movement could explode into full-scale revolt. Kimbangu himself tried to make clear that he did not have a political goal. But he was kept in prison or under arrest for almost thirty years, until his death in 1951. He came to be regarded as a martyr by many Africans, and his church is still an active organization with thousands of members.

7. The twentieth century has brought many changes to the Muslim world in the Middle East. Though there are differences among Muslims, their life bears witness to the continuing role of religion in today's world.

The Muslim nations of the Middle East have undergone many political changes since World War I. Out of the old Ottoman Empire, Turkey emerged as an independent republic in 1923. Its leader was Mustafa Kemal (1881-1939), later named Atatürk (Father of the Turks). As president of Turkey, Atatürk exercised sole and supreme authority. Sweeping constitutional changes turned Turkey into what seemed to be a Western-style nation.

Islam lost many of its privileges as the official state religion. The Western calendar and the Roman alphabet were adopted, replacing the Arabic calendar and alphabet. Women received the right to vote and to hold office and much greater opportunity.

Some Turks think that the process of nationalism, modernization, and westernization went too far. They complain that the Muslim religion has lost its rightful place in the life of Turks.

In the Arab world, French and English protectorates gave way to independent countries in which the influence of Islam remained strong. Some muslims hoped to bring about Arab unity and to make Islam the chief worldwide religion. Some wished to keep Islam separate from political and civil life. Others preferred to reject all Western influence and stick to strict Muslim doctrine.

Though Iran is not an Arab country, its main religion is Islam. Much modernization had taken place in Iran during the twentieth century, much of it under the rule of Reza Shah Pahlavi, who ruled from 1925 to 1941. His son, Mohammed Pahlavi Reza, became the Shah of Iran in 1942 and ruled until 1979. The United States from the west and Russia from the north exerted much political pressure on Iran during his reign. But the demands of strict Muslim leaders and dissatisfaction with the totalitarian rule of the Shah brought about a revolution in 1979. Iranians overthrew the Shah, and their religious leader, the Ayatollah Khomeini, became political leader also. The new regime was often as harsh toward people who criticized it as had been the rule of the Shah.

As this history shows, the religion of Islam still plays an important role in the lives of Muslims in many different countries. The issue of separation of church and state has not been settled in the Muslim countries, and Muslims still take this issue seriously.

Centuries of hostility and ignorance between Christians and Muslims still affect relations today. Western interest in controlling the oil reserves in the Middle East has also complicated current dealings with Muslims. But both Christians and Muslims believe that religion must examine and criticize trends in modern society in the light of serious belief in God and God's plan for the world.

There are sharp differences in religious views among Muslims as there are among Christians. This sometimes causes bitterness between various groups of Muslims and also shows how serious they are about their religion.

8. The twentieth century has brought both tragedy and hope to Judaism. The bigotry and persecution of centuries reached a horrible climax in the Holocaust (1933-1945). The new Jewish nation of Israel was created in Palestine in 1948.

Several million Jews immigrated to the United States in the late 1800s and early 1900s. They were fleeing from poverty, hatred, and murder in Christian lands of eastern Europe. Although the United States was free from the worst forms of persecution, many American Roman Catholics and Protestants, even among the clergy, expressed anti-Jewish feelings during these years.

Christian Europe had a history of anti-Jewish feeling. Forgetting that Jesus had died for the sins of all people, Christians sometimes unjustly blamed Jews for his death, calling them "Christ-killers." Such traditions made it easier for Christians to sit back when Jews were persecuted. The climax of persecution came in the Holocaust (1933-1945), described in chapter 14. This wholesale killing of Jews was begun by Nazi leaders of Germany. But some Europeans who were neither Nazi nor German helped the Nazis to round up Jews, or did not object when Jews were arrested and sent away to be killed. Some Christians were jealous of the remarkable achievements and prosperity of some Jews. Today many Christians are still concerned about how deeply

anti-Semitism has been imbedded in Christianty.

However, there were many brave individuals and groups who did try to help the Jews. For example, Raoul Wallenberg, a Swedish diplomat, reportedly saved as many as 100,000 Jews in Budapest, Hungary, in 1944.

Jews have played an important role in modern thought and culture. Examples are physicist Albert Einstein, whose theories have been important in the development of atomic energy; Sigmund Freud, the father of modern psychology; writers Franz Kafka and Isaac Bashevis Singer; composers Gustav Mahler and Leonard Bernstein; and entertainers Groucho Marx and Woody Allen.

Theodore Herzl (1860-1904), a Jewish journalist, was shocked by anti-Jewish feelings and actions in France. He founded Zionism, the movement to establish a Jewish nation in

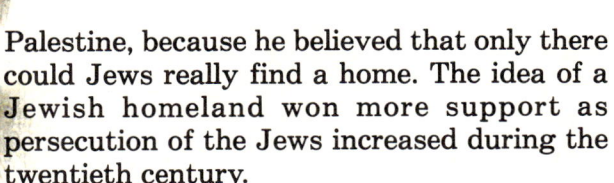

Palestine, because he believed that only there could Jews really find a home. The idea of a Jewish homeland won more support as persecution of the Jews increased during the twentieth century.

(Pictured at right bottom is Hitler, the anti-Jewish German dictator; and at top right, the leaders of the nations that defeated Germany in World War II.)

The Jewish state of Israel came into existence in 1948, after the end of the war. Jews from throughout the world, many of them survivors of the Nazi persecutions, have immigrated to Israel to start a new life.

Unresolved is the problem of the many Arabs who also claim Palestine as their homeland. As early as 1921 Martin Buber called upon Jews and Arabs to create a nation where "both peoples will have the opportunity to develop freely." That goal remains unrealized, and several times war has broken out between Israel and its neighbor Muslim nations. President Anwar Sadat of Egypt made serious efforts to establish relations with Israel before he was killed in 1981. But some other Arab leaders continue to deny the right of a Jewish state to exist.

9. In Mexico, revolutionary governments tried to bring about social reforms. Often these forces were hostile to the Roman Catholic Church and instigated persecutions. The Mexican people, for most part, remained loyal to the Catholic Church.

A revolutionary atmosphere existed in Mexico in the early part of the twentieth century. Some of the new leaders who came to power were hostile to the Catholic clergy and the role of the Catholic Church in Mexican life. In 1914 Venustiano Carranza came to power. Opposed to the Church, he favored land reform, better conditions for labor, and more opportunities for the common people. Many priests and Catholics worked actively for reform. However, some large landowners were Catholic lay people or priests, and they opposed land reform and other measures which would undermine the privileged position they enjoyed.

In 1917 a new constitution proclaimed national ownership of all lands, waters, and mineral resources. It promised an eight-hour day to workers and forbade child labor. It also brought into force various anti-clerical laws. Places of worship became the property of the state. The Catholic Church was forbidden to operate schools. Priests were not allowed to vote, to hold public office, or to criticize the government and its laws. Some official state governors did not bother to enforce these laws as strictly as others. But the laws remained in effect and were often used to justify persecution of the clergy, religious, and loyal lay Catholics.

There was strong public reaction against anti-Church measures as loyal Catholics organized to defend the Church. A monument dedicated to Christ the King in 1923 became the rallying point for armed revolt by the "Cristeros." Their slogan "Long live Christ the King" was echoed widely in Mexico. Clergy, religious, and lay people active in religion were persecuted, expelled from the country, or sometimes killed. One of the most well known victims of this persecution was the Mexican Jesuit, Father Miguel Pro, who was shot by a firing squad in 1927. Using a wide variety of disguises, he had gone about his priestly work in Mexico City, even visiting those imprisoned by the government.

The period of persecution ended around 1940. Since then the Catholic Church and its faithful have played an important role in Mexican life. Service to the Christian faith and to the Mexican people have gone hand in hand. The Catholic heirarchy has spoken out for social justice, and the Church has attempted to identify more forcefully with the poor of Mexico.

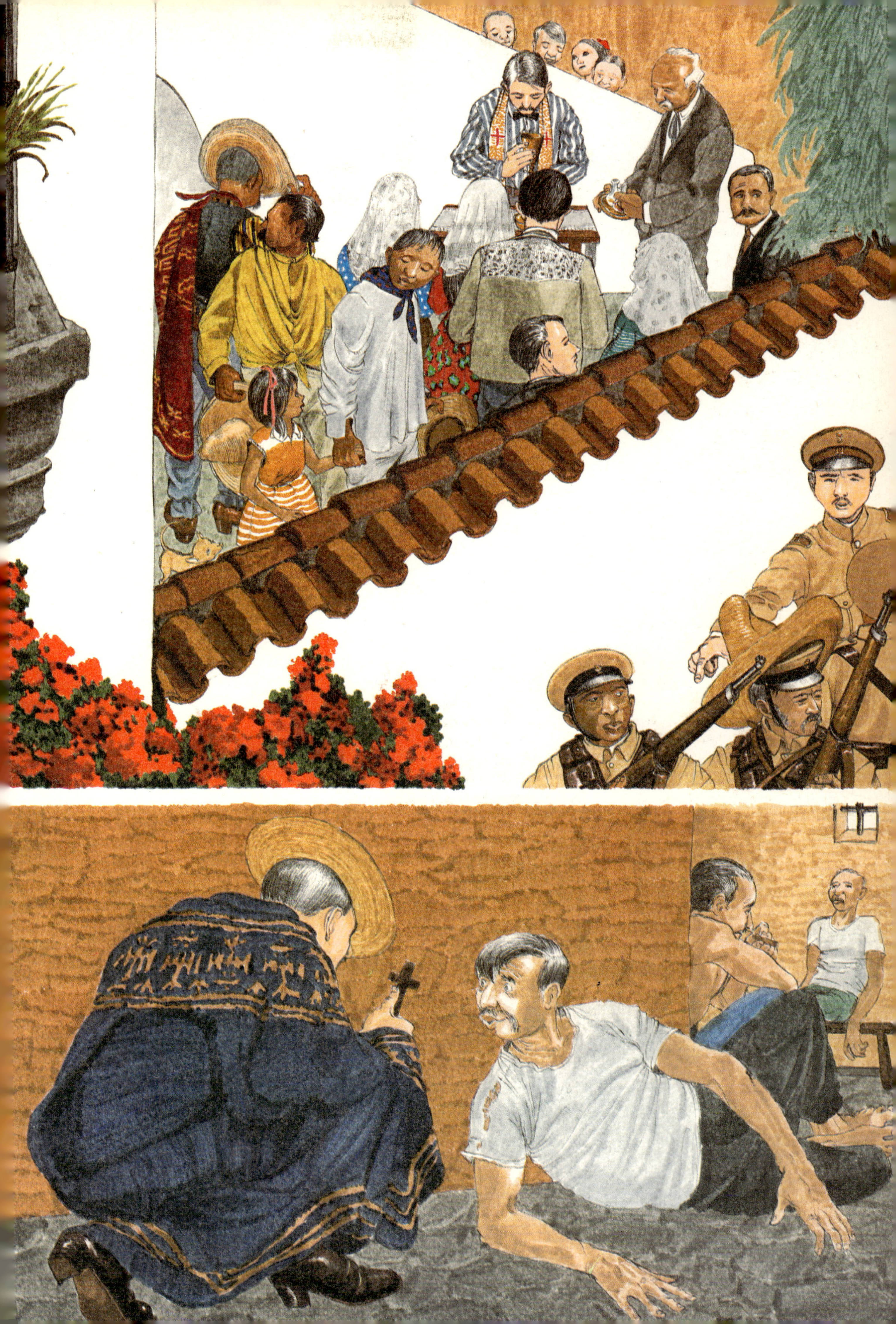

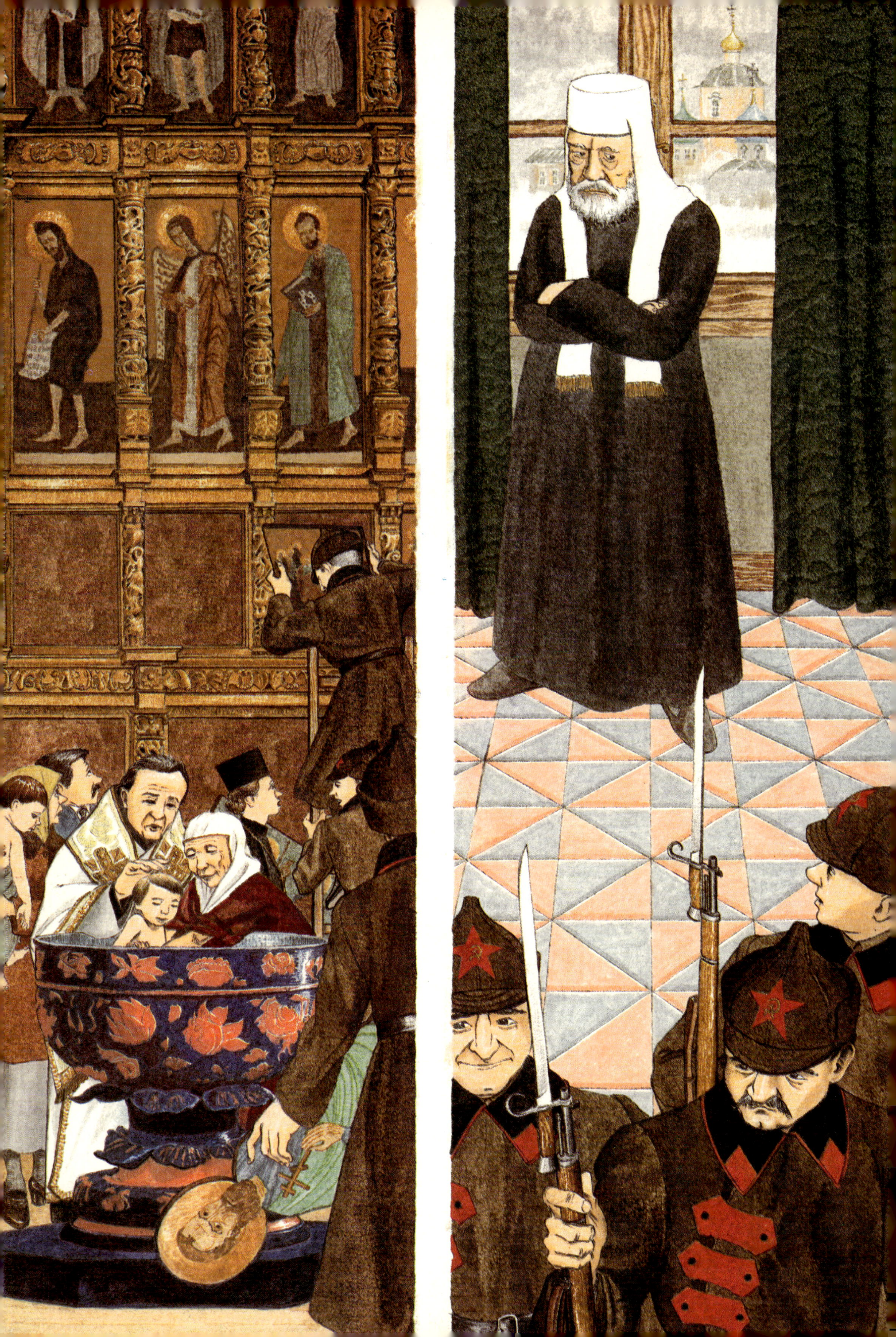

10. The Russian Orthodox Church was persecuted under Communist rule in the years following the Russian revolution. Churches were destroyed or closed, and atheism was taught in schools.

In March, 1917, a revolution overthrew the Russian czar and established a shaky democracy. The following October, the Bolsheviks, a group of radical Communists, seized power. The Communist Party, under the leadership of Nikolai Lenin (1870-1924), took control of Russia. Persons who questioned the government were removed from public life and sent to prison camps or executed. During the 1920s and 1930s, millions of Russian people were killed.

The government established a system of production based on communistic principles. It was applied very strictly, but it did not increase production of goods. In fact, the new system seemed to hurt rather than help production. By 1921, Lenin began to bring back some of the features of the capitalistic system, in which one or a few people managed production, instead of having all the workers manage it, which was the Communist ideal.

The Orthodox Church was also affected, because the new Bolshevik rulers were convinced atheists. They saw religion as foolish and old-fashioned, and they wanted belief in God to be removed from people's lives. Churches, monasteries, and icons (a kind of religious picture) were to disappear. Prayer and religious practices were to be stamped out. Russia was to develop new Communist human beings who lived by science and reason. History was interpreted as the struggle among social classes.

The rulers of the Soviet Union, as the Communists now called the nation, followed this program strictly and ruthlessly. They used all the new techniques of communication and education to force this program on the people: newspapers, books, films, classrooms, and so forth. Dividing people from one another by fear, they were able to insure their own power and prevent the rise of popular protest. Yet the opposition was there, though hidden and secretive.

The Bolsheviks dealt viciously with the Russian Orthodox Church. They robbed crypts and churches. They took church funds and nationalized parochial schools. They killed lay people, priests, and religious after fake trials or without any trials at all. The head of the Russian Orthodox Church was put under house arrest. Many intellectuals and theologians were driven out of the country, or managed to escape on their own. Jews and Muslims, as well as Christians, were objects of Communist persecution.

The new Bolshevik state paid particular attention to teaching the new principles of Communism to children from an early age. The government tried to undermine the love and loyalty of children toward their parents and relatives. Bitter propaganda against God, religion, and church life filled the schools.

Joseph Stalin (1879-1953), dictator of the Soviet Union from 1926 to 1953, lessened persecution of the Russian Church in order to unite the country during the war against Germany (1939-1945). But he was a ruthless person, responsible for the imprisonment and death of millions of his fellow Russians.

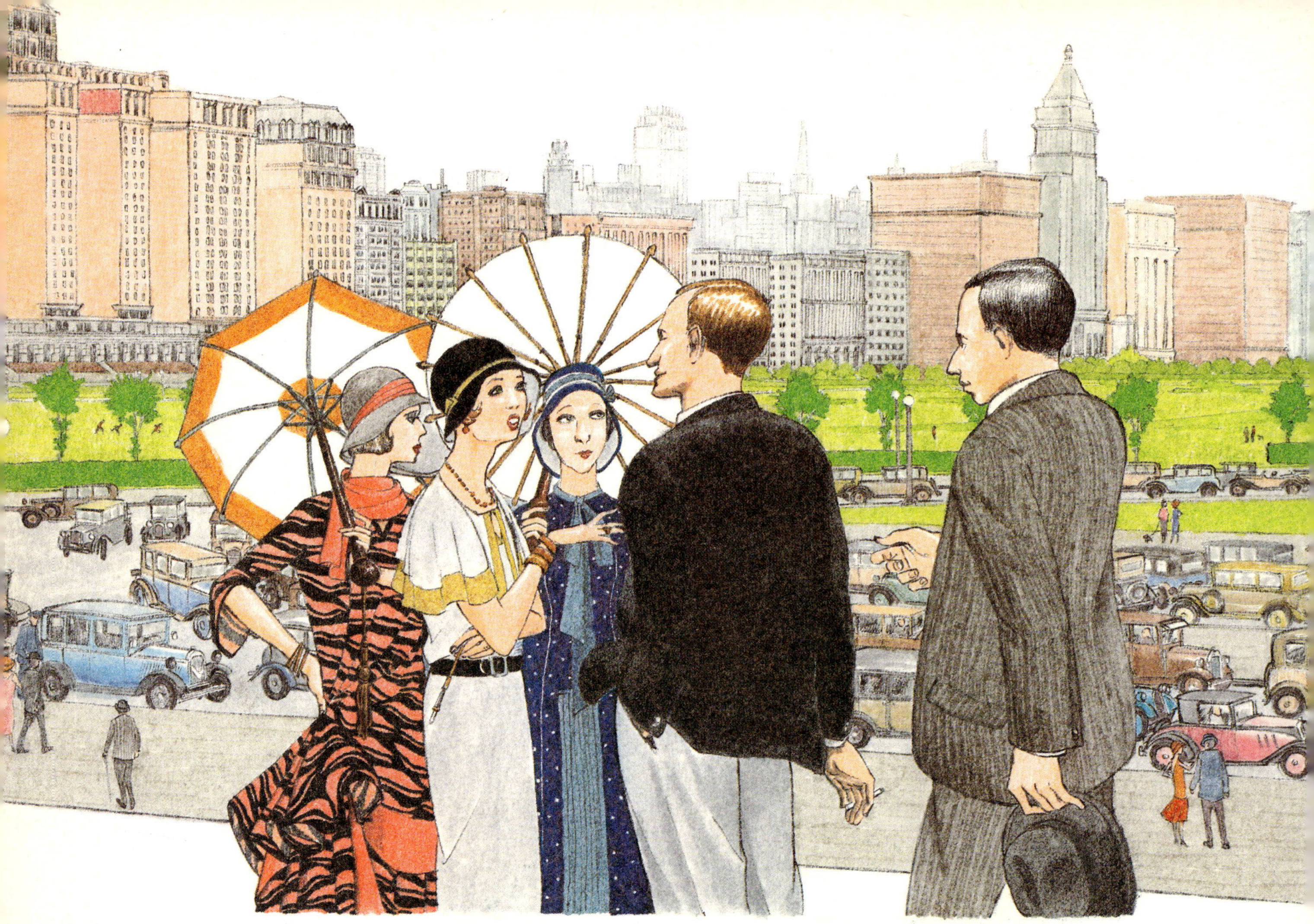

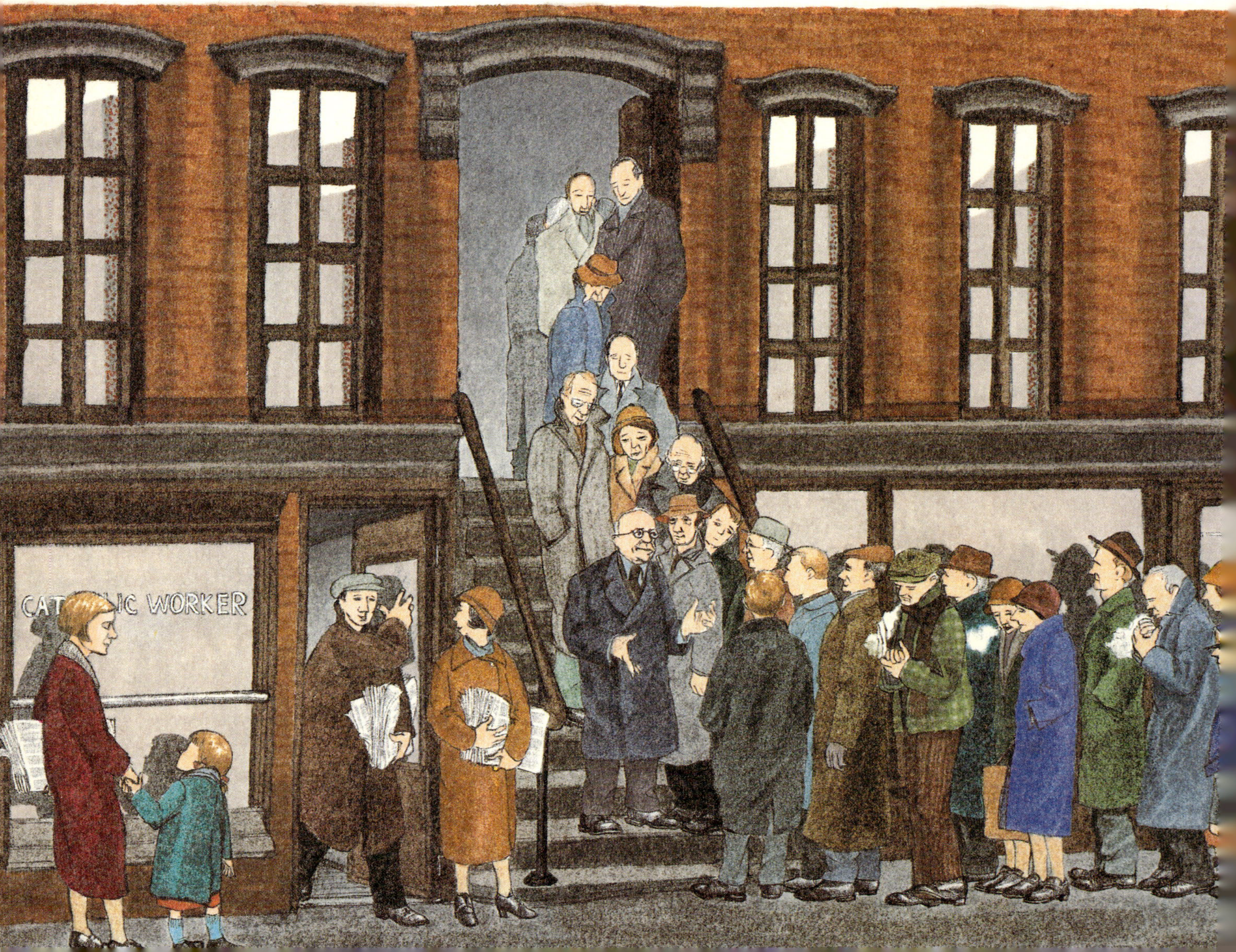

CAT LIC WORKER

11. In the United States, the beginning of the U.S. Catholic Conference and the work of Dorothy Day were signs of the growing spirit of community in the Catholic Church.

During World War I, an organization called the National Catholic War Council had been formed to bring together the efforts of several Roman Catholic groups to help servicemen and war victims. After the war, Father John J. Burke, the founder, and some American bishops wanted to continue the Council. They recognized that a national organization was a good way for Catholic diocesan and parish groups to combine their efforts toward solving social problems.

As a result, the National Catholic Welfare Conference (NCWC) came into being in 1919. The Conference handled many matters besides social work. For example, it set up a news service for diocesan newspapers. Also, national policies for Catholic schools now began to be established by the Conference.

The NCWC also became deeply involved with social issues, under the leadership of its first director, Monsignor John A. Ryan. Soon after it was founded, NCWC issued a statement calling for recognition of labor unions, for industry to share its profits with workers, and for equal wages for men and women who did equal work.

The National Catholic Welfare Conference continues its work today under the name United States Catholic Conference (USCC), which it took in 1966.

Another movement of special and continuing importance was the Catholic Worker movement, founded by Peter Maurin (1877-1947) and Dorothy Day (1897-1980). Maurin was a French worker-thinker who tried to work out the ideals of a social order where the image of God might be really mirrored in the lives of people. Dorothy Day was a journalist and former Socialist who became a Roman Catholic. She was eager to prove false the Communist claim that the Church was not concerned with the welfare of workers.

On May Day (May 1) 1933, Dorothy Day published the first issue of her monthly newspaper, *The Catholic Worker*. It cost one penny a copy, and was still sold at that price in 1982. *The Catholic Worker* explores the real-life meaning of the gospel message and the social teachings of the Roman Catholic Church.

The Catholic Worker Movement tackled the sufferings of the poor and out-of-work. At that time, the United States was in the Great Depression. Millions of people were unemployed, and had no way to buy food and other necessities of life. Dorothy Day opened soup kitchens, hospitality houses, and farm communities. She supported labor, social justice, and peace.

Dorothy Day asked that the members of her movement lead lives of prayer, self-denial, and participation in the sacraments. Many priests, religious, and lay people worked at her Catholic Worker centers across the nation and helped spread her influence throughout the American Catholic Church.

In her biography, *The Long Loneliness*, Dorothy Day described her work: "The most significant thing about the Catholic Worker is poverty, some say...community, others say... But the final word is love...We cannot love God unless we love each other, and to love we must know each other...We have all known the long loneliness and we have learned that the only solution is love, and that love comes with community."

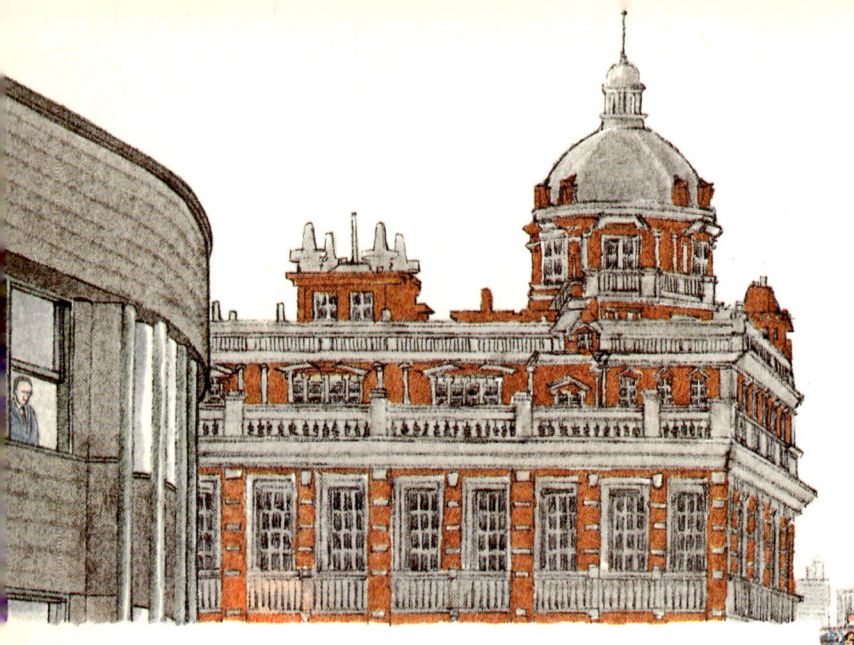

12. The Church worked to improve conditions for working people in large metropolises.

Cities all over the world continued to grow in the years after World War I, and some European city dwellers began to write and speak longingly of the more peaceful life of the countryside. Others yearned to return to the Middle Ages, when almost all of Europe was united in one Christian Church. It was easy to idealize the Middle Ages, imagining the people who lived then had no problems. But historians could point out that in those times, as in the present, there were crime, poor government, and oppression of workers.

In the 1920s in the big cities of European countries, such as France, the Roman Catholic Church was no longer in close contact with the people. Some people were hostile to religion and some others were completely uninterested in it.

In the Roman Catholic Church in the United States during this time, the majority of priests and bishops had a friendly, close relationship with the people. This was partly because a large majority of the clergy were from working class families. With this background, it was natural that a number of Roman Catholic clergy in the 1920s and 1930s would become social activists and try to help workers improve their conditions. (A "social activist" is a person who takes action to solve a problem in society.)

The Catholic Church is traditionally associated with city life. In the 1930s, most large cities in the United States had their "labor priests," as priests who devoted themselves to helping workers were called. They were consultants and spiritual advisors. Also, they established courses to teach the social encyclicals of the popes. These teachings included Pope Leo XIII's letter *On the Condition of Working People* (1891) and Pius XI's letter forty years later, called *Renewal of the Social Order,* which supported the rights of working people.

Racial segregation and discrimination added to the problems of large American cities. A number of Roman Catholics worked to improve relations between the Roman Catholic Church and black Americans. One of these people was John LaFarge, a Jesuit, who started the first Catholic Interracial Council. Another was Bishop Bernard Sheil of Chicago. He was a friend of labor unions and worked tirelessly for civil rights and desegregation, and to clear the slums. Bishop Sheil began the Catholic Youth Organization (CYO) to organize sports and social programs for Catholic parishes.

A lay woman who worked selflessly for social justice was Catherine de Hueck. A Russian baroness, she came to America after World War I to escape the Russian revolution. She began settlement houses where the poor and homeless could come for help. Her first house was in Toronto, Ontario, and houses were also established in Chicago, Washington, D.C., and New York. Her center in Harlem, New York, called Friendship House, worked to eliminate segregation and to promote interracial programs.

13. The Bauhaus of Germany became an important influence on architecture in the United States and in Europe.

In the later 1800s and early 1900s, a new type of building called a skyscraper became more and more popular in large cities. These tall buildings were made possible by the use of steel for construction and by the invention of the elevator for traveling from floor to floor inside. Skyscrapers were usually built very close to each other, so that business people could work together more easily. As a result, city land became very expensive.

Many skyscrapers were very beautiful, as architects created new designs to work with modern materials. Frank Lloyd Wright (1869-1959) was one of the greatest architects of the century. He artistically adapted his buildings to their settings and showed great creativity in his work. A famous example of a Frank Lloyd Wright home is "Falling Water" (built in 1936-1937) in Bear Run, Pennsylvania.

In Germany, a new school of art called the Bauhaus was founded in 1919 by Walter Gropius. (Bauhaus means "house of architecture.") The artists Paul Klee and Vasily Kandinsky were among the teachers at the Bauhaus. This school attempted to combine study of arts with crafts. According to the Bauhaus, everything manufactured by people —buildings, furniture, dishes—should be designed so that it would fulfill its particular function in the most efficient way possible. The proportions of the finished object and the natural finish of its materials were to be the decoration—no other ornamentation was needed. This approach to design is called "functionalism" and was developed by Bauhaus. Steel furniture and tubular lighting are among Bauhaus productions.

In 1933, the Bauhaus was closed by the German government, which was then controlled by the Nazi party. A few years later—1939— the Chicago Institute of Design was founded by Laszlo Moholy-Nagy, a Hungarian who had taught at the Bauhaus. The design of American commercial and industrial buildings and other works was greatly influenced by this school.

Some Bauhaus designs have been criticized. Some critics say that recent office buildings are little more than "glass boxes," and that they do not fit in well with their surroundings. Nevertheless, Bauhaus designs continue to be used for things as simple as tea kettles and for enterprises as complex as shopping centers.

14. Totalitarian rule came to Germany under Adolf Hitler in 1933. Some other European nations also became dictatorships during the 1930s.

The terrible war of 1914-1918 and the harsh peace treaty placed great burdens on the new German democratic republic which was created in 1918. Incredible inflation and a high rate of unemployment made life in Germany very difficult. Many Germans had little interest in or respect for the new democratic government, called the Weimar Republic. Because Germany did not have a long history as a democracy, many of the German people did not expect a great deal from parliament or political parties.

The German school system did not help build respect for politics. It tended to foster a longing for the good old days, when rural life, duty, and soldier-like obedience to country were the highest ideals. During this time after World War I, many Germans were attracted by a mass movement which appealed to their patriotism and nationalism. This movement was called National Socialism, and became known as the Nazi party. Its head was Adolf Hitler (1889-1945).

Hitler promised prosperity. National socialism appealed especially to workers. Working people were described as soldiers in the service of their country. Nevertheless, no one particular group made up the Nazi party. In 1932 Nazis included, among others, workers, disillusioned veterans, factory owners, teachers, farmers, politicians, and members of the Prussian military aristocracy.

In 1933, the Nazis won in a free election. But Germany quickly became a dictatorship. Under the Nazi regime, newspapers were no longer free to publish their views openly. Universities were no longer independent of government control.

The Nazi government had a policy of persecuting the Jewish citizens of Germany. Mobs destroyed synagogues and stores owned by Jews, and police did not try to stop their crimes. In 1935, the Nazi government took away the citizenship of German Jews. The German government had a plan to kill all the Jews. Nazis called this plan "the final solution," a phrase which encouraged Germans to see Jews as a problem.

Jews were arrested and put into huge prison camps called concentration camps. Thousands of German Jews were moved to the camps. They suffered greatly and most of them were killed. In the following years, as Nazi Germany conquered and occupied Poland, France, and other countries, they continued to round up and kill the Jews. Six million Jews, more than half the Jews in Europe, were killed. This terrible period of mass murder is called the Holocaust.

Both the Protestant and Roman Catholic Churches spoke out against Nazi policy when it clashed with articles of faith, or threatened church interests or organizations. But many German Christians now feel that they did not do enough to oppose Nazi crimes against the Jews and against human rights in general.

Feelings of fear and helplessness can prevent people from speaking out against wrongs or acting according to their principles. It seems safer to be quiet. After World War II, one Protestant clergyman, Martin Niemoeller, who did finally stand up to Adolf Hitler, put it this way: "When the Nazis came to get the Communists, I was silent. When they came to get the Socialists, I was silent. When they came to get the Catholics, I was silent. When they came to get the Jews, I was silent. And when they came to get me, there was no one left to speak."

Between the two world wars Spain and Italy also became dictatorships. Italy kept its king in name, but in 1922 Benito Mussolini (1883-1945) became dictator. In Spain a revolution overthrew the monarchy in 1931 and a bloody civil war (1936-1939) followed. At its end, Francisco Franco (1892-1975) became dictator of Spain. Russia had become a dictatorship after the revolution of 1917. Thus, by the late 1930s, much of Europe was under totalitarian rule.

USSR

MANCHURIA

Beijing

Seoul

KOREA

Nanjing

Shanghai

CHINA

Hong Kong

Macao

15. In China during the 1920s and the 1930s, there was warfare between Communists and the government. In Japan during these years the situation for Christianity became more and more dangerous because Japan's rulers regarded the Church as something foreign and anti-Japanese.

Important political changes took place in the Far East between the two world wars. These changes had an impact on the life of the Christian churches in the area.

China had become a republic in 1912 under the Kuomintang Party, but it was not at peace within. Europeans and Americans continued to have economic and political interests in China, giving support to various warlords who were opposing the republic. Sun Yat-Sen (1866-1925), the president of the republic, exercised power mainly in southern China. The influence of the Bolshevik revolution in Russia was felt in China. The Chinese Communist Party was founded in 1921, and Sun Yat-sen had ties with the Soviets. In 1927, however, General Chiang Kai-shek (1887-1975) overthrew the government and established one hostile to Communism. There was warfare between his supporters and the Communists, and in 1935, the Communists were on the verge of total defeat. But the Red Army, under the strategic leadership of Mao Zedong (1893-1976), found safety in the north after its Long March of 10,000 kilometers (6,000 miles). There they established a soviet republic.

Amid all these upsetting events, the Protestant and Catholic churches barely managed to carry on. Maryknoll, an American order of foreign missionaries, had sent many priests and nuns to China. Efforts were increased to ensure a native Chinese Catholic Church. After a national Catholic synod in Shanghai in 1924, native Chinese clergy began to be more in charge of Chinese parishes and dioceses. Because Chiang Kai-shek was a Christian and opposed communism, many Christians supported him despite corruption of his government.

Japan was much stronger after World War I. It now held all the former German possessions in the Far East and the Pacific region. It also had many economic privileges in China, and so it was the most important Asian power. It soon began to expand in China, first in Manchuria and then in Mongolia, Beijing, Shanghai, and Nanjing. Japan's own democratic government was soon taken over by the military with its dreams of glory and expansion. Dangerous ideas were to be eliminated by censorship, police tactics, and murder. Political parties were crushed. Shinto reverence for the state and the emperor went hand in hand with ideas of the Japanese as a superior race.

The situation for Christianity became more dangerous than before in Japan. It was regarded as something foreign and anti-Japanese. To make life easier for the Catholic Church in Japan, its foreign bishops decided to resign their posts in 1940 and let Japanese Christians take their place. That same year the Japanese government required heads of all Christian churches and schools to be Japanese. When World War II came, Japanese armies overran many parts of Asia in which Christian world missions had been operating.

16. In France, various thinkers sought to remind Christians of their responsibility to face the problems of the modern world. Emmanuel Mounier and Jacques Maritain were very important influences in this movement.

The Catholic Church had lost contact with many people in the modern cities of Europe. Christianity was no longer the bond of unity and community that it once had been. To many people it seemed unimportant as an influence in social life. The crises in people's lives seemed beyond Christian control.

In France, as in other parts of Europe, various people and movements arose to tackle the problem. They tried to give Christians a greater sense of responsibility for the world around them. The Christian faith, they insisted, was not a matter of private belief alone. It meant responsibility for the surrounding world as well. One vigorous spokesman for lively practice of the faith in the modern world was Emmanuel Mounier (1905-1950). Founder of the school of thought known as "personalism," Mounier was an active Roman Catholic who pleaded for a new social order, but who never ceased to stress the deeper mystery of human life and history. His many writings in the journal which he founded, *Esprit*, influenced a wide variety of people ranging from Roman Catholics to Marxists. Mounier denounced greed and materialism, stressing human dignity and the importance of the relationship between human beings and God. The philosopher Nietzsche had attacked Christians as weaklings, and Mounier urged

Christians to show by their actions that only Christianity had the generosity and strength to make the world truly human.

Another group of writers and thinkers gathered around Jacques Maritain (1882-1973) and his wife, Raïssa. Besides his important work in exploring and presenting the thought of Thomas Aquinas, Maritain tried to offer a Christian view of "integral humanism." True humanism in the full sense, he said, must come from Christian principles that are put into practice in every area of life. Even in our own times, such figures as the late Eduardo Frei, the former president of Chile, believed that Maritain's view of integral humanism has much to contribute to better democratic politics.

It is important to realize that the activity of such figures was surrounded and supported by the work of many other groups who were seeking to revive Catholic intellectual and spiritual life. The fine historian of philosophy, Étienne Gilson, showed the value and importance of medieval philosophy and theology. And various church movements tried to involve lay people in the church and the world as active Christians.

Catholic Action was an effort to create a structure of lay activity under the guidance of the hierarchy. Pius XI has been called the Pope of Catholic Action for his efforts in this area. He wanted to see groups of dedicated lay men and women in every parish, ranging from young people to adults. He hoped they would be backed up by diocesan organizations and similar groups in schools and universities. These organizations would help Catholics to see new opportunities to live the Christian life in an active way, to carry the Christian message and example into everyday work and leisure. Being a Christian was a fulltime task, not something to be done only on Sundays or in church. In general, Catholic Action was effective among people who retained solid ties to the Church, but it was not so successful in areas where people had lost contact with their faith. Yet it helped make lay people aware of their Christian task.

17. Pius XI tried to protect Catholics by entering into concordats with the governments of Italy and Germany. The agreement with the Italian government made Vatican City an independent state.

to make concordats with various existing governments.

Pius XI made an important concordat with the Italian government that is still in effect and that enabled the Roman Catholic Church to settle a long-lasting problem. Up until 1870, a large section of Italy had been controlled by the pope, but the Italian government had taken over these regions when Italy became a unified nation. Pius XI realized that there was no point in continuing to demand the return of these lands. He wanted to make an agreement which would end any conflict in the consciences of Italian Catholics between supporting their nation and supporting their Church.

The Italian government, now headed by Benito Mussolini (1883-1945), was also interested in such an agreement for its own political reasons. Talks began in 1926 and in

The Christian presence of the Roman Catholic Church in society was a lifelong concern of Pope Pius XI. He wanted the Church to influence other social institutions with the spirit of Christianity. To do this, the pope tried

1929 an agreement was signed. The papacy recognized the kingdom of Italy with Rome as its capital. The Italian government recognized the sovereign authority of the pope over a small piece of territory in Rome which came to be known as Vatican City. A financial agreement was also reached. The Italian government was to pay the Vatican a sum of money in return for the territories which the papacy had lost.

Another concordat was made between the papacy and the Nazi government in Germany. Signed in 1933, it seemed to be very beneficial to the Catholic Church. In fact, Adolf Hitler and the Nazi government ignored it.

Pius XI has been criticized for making these concordats with Italy and Germany. It is said that he helped to give political respectability to fascism and Nazism by recognizing such governments. It is possible that the pope was too hopeful about the beneficial results of such concordats. But documents and testimony from that period suggest that the pope was not greatly deceived by the Nazi government or its promises. The concordat was merely an attempt by formal, legal means to protect Roman Catholics from the harshness of the Nazi regime.

18. Protestant theology flourished after World War II. Rudolf Bultmann tried to remove myth from the Bible. Leonhard Ragaz founded the movement of religious socialists. Paul Tillich attempted to reconcile religion and culture, and Reinhold Niebuhr tried to relate Christian ethics to an industrial society.

Between World War I and World War II, Christian thought was deepened by great theologians. Many of them were Protestants, but their thinking influenced both Protestants and Roman Catholics. The best known of these thinkers was Karl Barth (1886-1968). Born in Basel, Switzerland, he studied theology in the major German universities. In 1918 he published his famous commentary on the *Epistle to the Romans*. In it Barth opposed liberal theology and underlined God's greatness and God's self-revelation in Jesus Christ. God is totally different, said Barth, from human beings who must bow in faith and worship.

Rudolf Bultmann, another famous Protestant theologian, was a disciple of the existentialist philosopher Heidegger. Bultmann wanted to eliminate from the faith miracles and other supernatural elements. He thought these made Christianity difficult for modern persons to accept. The heart of Christian faith, Bultmann said, did not concern the life of Jesus, but the power he now brings to individual human lives. Bultmann called his program of revision "demythologizing."

Another Swiss theologian, Leonhard Ragaz, focused his thinking on the social dimensions of Christianity. In 1906 he founded the movement known as religious socialism. Ragaz devoted the rest of his life to organizing this movement.

Another major theologian was Paul Tillich (1886-1965). He believed that the starting point in theology should be the questions and needs of persons. Because of his opposition to Nazism, Tillich was forced to give up teaching in Germany. He came to the United States in 1933 at the invitation of his friend Reinhold Niebuhr, to teach at Union Theological Seminary in New York.

Niebuhr (1892-1971), probably the greatest modern American theologian, started as a pastor among assembly-line workers in Detroit. He tried to relate Christian ethics to complex, industrial society. One of his books, *Moral Man and Immoral Society*, shows that persons who are loving in personal relations may take part in very unjust social actions.

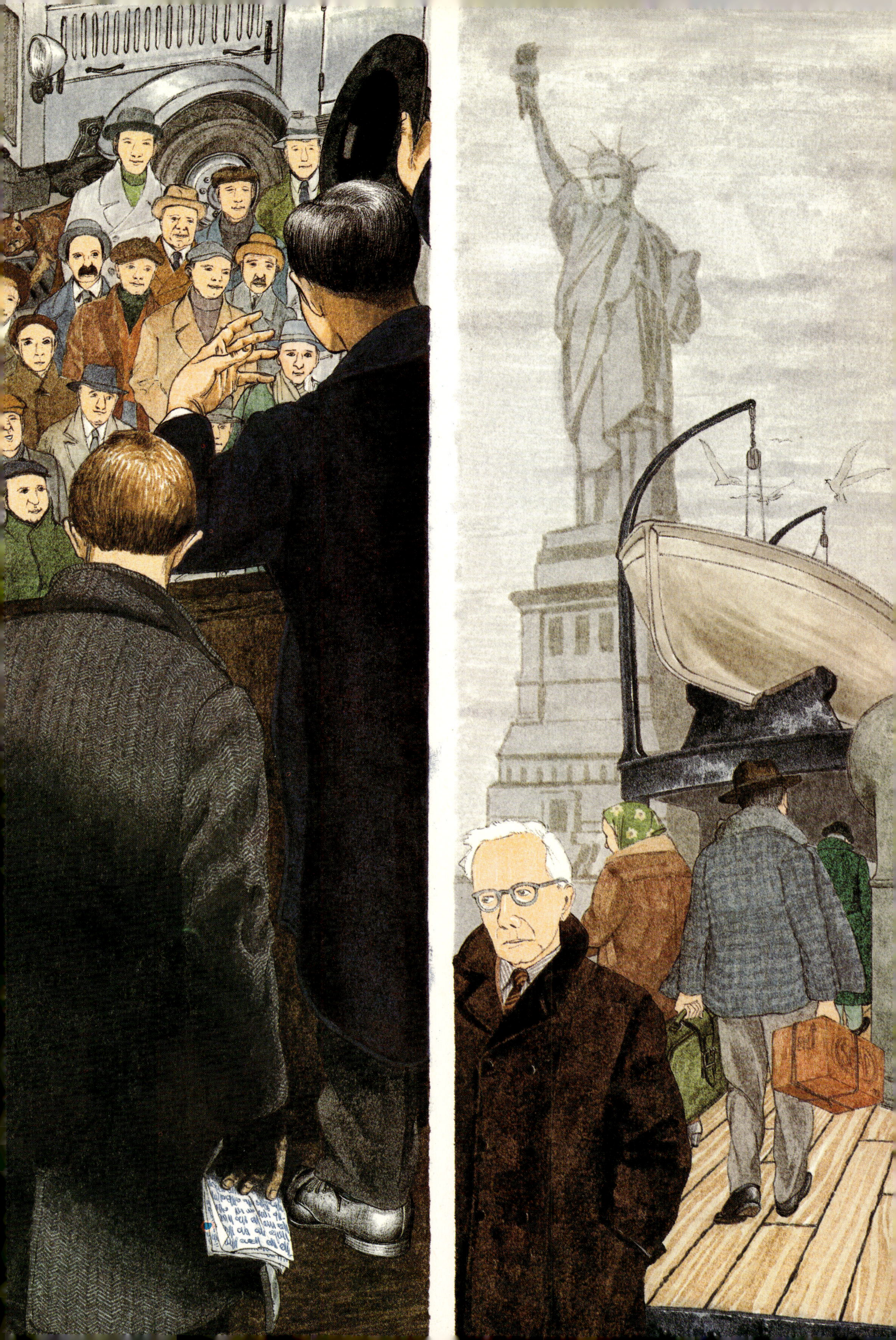

19. **The rise of Nazism was opposed by many Christians. At the request of Roman Catholic bishops, Pius XI condemned Nazism in 1935. In Protestant circles, the Confessing Church of Germany was established. This large group of churches joined to oppose Nazism. Many theology professors, such as Barth and Tillich, left their teaching posts at German universities in protest of Nazism.**

The Catholic Church had made the concordat with the Nazi German government as a means of defense against the threats of Nazism. However, both the pope and some German bishops, such as Faulhaber of Munich and Von Galen of Muenster realized that many Nazi doctrines, such as the belief that Germans were a superior race, were unacceptable from a human and Christian standpoint. Faced with Hitler's rise to power, the Roman Catholic Church wanted to protect itself. But only a few months after the concordat was signed, the Nazi government openly violated it. Many Catholic schools were turned into state schools, and other Catholic associations were disbanded.

The Vatican made repeated protests but they were unsuccessful. Five German bishops sponsored the idea of a public protest; from this idea came a papal encyclical against Nazism.

Italy, under Mussolini, was friendly with Hitler, and the pope could not issue the encyclical from Vatican City in Rome. Bishop

Francis Spellman, who later became a cardinal, visited the pope just when the encyclical was ready, and he smuggled it out of Italy in his luggage.

On March 21, 1937, the encyclical was read in all Catholic churches in Germany. No race and no people, said the encyclical, can violate the rights of the individual. The human being, "as a person, possesses God-given rights which must be safeguarded from any and every attack." The Nazi regime responded with harsh reprisals, including mock trials of priests and religious and efforts to draw the faithful away from their pastors. Nevertheless, the encyclical spoke plainly to the world and the German Church. It said in effect: The Church is in a life-and-death struggle; German Catholics who are suffering persecution are in the right.

The Protestant Churches of Germany were also unprepared for Hitler's rise to power. At first there was a current which favored Nazism. Some theologians and other Christians, however, quickly realized that Nazism and Christianity could not be reconciled. Theologians Karl Barth, Paul Tillich, and others, chose to lose their jobs rather than take an oath of loyalty to Hitler.

Some Protestants took part in the German Christian Movement sponsored by the Nazis, but the Confessing Church of Germany led Protestant resistance to the Nazi regime. Organized in Barmen in 1934 by seven thousand ministers, the Confessing Church published an open condemnation of Nazism as idolatry. Arrests and other forms of persecution then began. Martin Niemoeller and other leaders of the Confessing Church were placed in prisons called concentration camps. The best known leader was the theologian Dietrich Bonhoeffer. He was executed on April 9, 1945, a few days before the end of the war.

20. World War II (1939-1945)

During the 1930s, and especially after the Nazi party came into power in Germany in 1933, a second world war seemed certain to break out. In some countries, such as Japan, Russia, Germany, and Italy, national propaganda programs prepared for war by emphasizing the importance of military forces. But World War II grew out of the policies of governments rather than out of the feelings of common people. Governments wanted to gain more territory and to have control over areas of the world that had important raw materials needed for industry.

In 1939, Germany occupied Poland in a surprise move, and war began. Britain and France joined together to fight against Germany, and Italy entered the war on the German side. German forces occupied Denmark, Norway, Holland, Luxembourg, Belgium and, eventually, France. The war spread to the Balkans, then to Africa. In 1941, Germany invaded Russia and in December of that year, Japan attacked the United States. At this point, most of the countries of Europe, Asia, and Africa were involved in the war, and also, United States, Canada and Australia. Only a few neutral European countries and the Latin American nations were not involved.

The people in military forces suffered most during the war, and civilian populations also endured great suffering. In Europe, North Africa, India, Indo-China, China, and Japan, people were bombarded from sea and air. They lived through guerrilla warfare, occupations by invading and liberating forces, shortages of food, black-market activities, police law and forced labor. Jews in Europe also suffered the horror of being sent to death camps by the invading, victorious Germans.

In 1943, Italy gave up the conflict. Northern Italy remained occupied by the German army for almost two more years, and southern Italy was occupied by the United States and Britain. In the spring of 1945, the Allies were victorious in Europe. The following August, the war with Japan ended when the United States dropped two atomic bombs on the cities of Hiroshima and Nagasaki. The bombs killed 200,000 people and their radiation ruined the lives of many others. Japan surrendered within a few days.

Peace was welcomed with great joy. The destruction of the war had been terrible. Millions of people were living as refugees, trying to reunite their families and to find a place to live in peace. Until World War II, the United States had been somewhat isolationist in its policies, holding aloof from political involvement in Europe. But that ended with the war, and the United States became a world power.

Of the many technical inventions of World War II, the use of atomic power is the most important. Other developments are radar; rockets and the first jet planes; improved aircraft; improved submarines and other naval vessels; improved electronics and communications; increase in industrial production.

These inventions were further improved and greatly expanded for civilian, peacetime use in the years after World War II. For example, the type for this book was set by electronic means, resulting from inventions made in the World War II era. Unfortunately, many World War II inventions continue to be used to prepare weapons that may lead to another war.

21. Pius XII was the head of the Roman Catholic Church during World War II. While pleading for peace, he attempted to follow a diplomatic course of action, convinced that this would help protect Catholics under Nazi rule. During Pius XII's papacy, the college of cardinals was greatly expanded.

On March 2, 1939, after a short conclave, Cardinal Eugenio Pacelli was elected pope and took the name Pius XII. Born in Rome in 1876, Pacelli had attended the best schools and universities in the capital and won the highest honors. Ordained a priest in 1899, he soon joined the Roman curia and became known for his intelligence and ability. In 1917 he was appointed nuncio to Munich, in 1925 nuncio to Berlin. In 1929 he was appointed a cardinal, and the next year he became papal secretary of state. Thus he worked very closely with Pius XI and directed Vatican policy, particularly in its dealings with Germany. To the cardinals he seemed to be the person most capable of confronting the coming war.

Right after his election, Pius XII spoke out against the threatening war, and made diplomatic contacts in an attempt to prevent the catastrophe; but all his efforts were in vain. By the end of 1939 the war was in progress, and it soon took on worldwide dimensions. Faced with the war, the pope increased his appeals for peace. In his Christmas messages during the war years, in particular, he spoke repeatedly about the conditions required to achieve a lasting international peace. These messages were backed up by diplomatic efforts to pacify the parties at war.

In the years following World War II, many people criticized Pius XII for not denouncing Nazi crimes with greater force and clarity. It seems certain, however, that the pope followed a more diplomatic course of action because he was convinced that this helped protect millions of Catholics living under Nazi rule.

The pope's work during World War II was more successful in the area of aid and assistance. The Vatican organized an information bureau to provide families with information about prisoners of war. This work benefited many people, but it faced great difficulties since Germany and Russia refused to participate in it. The Vatican also organized a committee to give aid and comfort to all those being persecuted.

Many persecuted people, Jews in particular, took refuge in the Vatican. Vatican convoys scoured Italy to find foodstuffs for the needy refugees.

Despite the war, the pope did not neglect his pastoral ministry. In 1943 he published two encyclicals that were very important for the life of the Church. His encyclical *Mystici corporis* urged the faithful to see the Church as the body of Christ. His encyclical *Divino afflante spiritu* encouraged deeper study of Sacred Scripture. Finally, it should be recalled that Pius XII played a decisive role in making the college of cardinals more universal by greatly increasing the total number and including people from many nations.

22. Nazism ruthlessly tried to destroy all persons of Jewish origin, and also claimed victims among Christians. Dietrich Bonhoeffer, a Protestant theologian, and Maximilian Kolbe, a Polish priest, gave up their lives in concentration camps, bearing witness to Christ.

Nazism and World War II cast a dark shadow over our own century and all human history. Nevertheless, there were people who, despite their pain and suffering, were not overwhelmed by evil. Several women come to mind. Anne Frank, a Jewish teenager, who died in the Holocaust, recorded in her diary her great love for life. Edith Stein, a Jewish scholar and a Catholic convert, was killed by the Nazis. She left moving reflections on the meaning of life and suffering. Many Christians struggled to protect Jews from Nazi persecution; one of these, Corrie ten Boom, a Dutch Protestant, has written several books about her experience.

Here we would like to say more about two Christian martyrs. Dietrich Bonhoeffer, a Protestant minister, and Maximilian Kolbe, a Polish priest.

Dietrich Bonhoeffer was born in Breslau on February 4, 1904. His family belonged to the upper middle class of Germany. His father was the director of a hospital, and everyone expected Dietrich to follow in his footsteps. But in 1923 Dietrich decided to become a minister and began his study of theology. In 1927 he received his degree and began an academic career, but he also did pastoral work. When Hitler came to power in 1933, Bonhoeffer was one of the first to foresee the effects of anti-Semitic legislation and to oppose the Nazi regime. He stopped teaching at the university and became director of an underground seminary belonging to the Confessing Church. During these years he wrote important works in theology. Although earlier in his life he had been a pacifist, Bonhoeffer now made contact with a political resistance movement which was plotting to kill Hitler. Discovered, Bonhoeffer was arrested and imprisoned. He was executed on April 9, 1945, just a few days before the end of World War II. Bonhoeffer's gravestone in a church in Flossenburg tells us that he chose to be "a witness to Jesus Christ among his brethren."

A few years earlier a Catholic priest, Maximilian Kolbe, gave the same sort of witness to Christ. Born in Poland in 1895 Kolbe became a Franciscan priest and dedicated his life to publishing. He was convinced that this was a new way to carry to humanity the message of Christ. The German invasion of Poland interrupted this work. Father Kolbe offered his services to a Red Cross hospital. In February 1941 he was arrested and imprisoned in the terrible concentration camp known as Auschwitz. While he and other prisoners were at work one day in July of that year, a prisoner escaped. As punishment for the escape of one prisoner, Nazi guards chose ten prisoners to be killed by starvation. Father Kolbe was not one of the ten chosen. But the desperation of a Polish soldier who had been chosen for death moved Father Kolbe. He called the German commandant and offered to die in place of the Polish soldier. Together with the other condemned prisoners, Father Kolbe was thrown into an underground vault, where he died on August 14, 1941. He had offered an example of both human and Christian love. In recognition of this love, in 1982 John Paul II declared Father Kolbe a saint.

23. Existentialism, a movement that can be traced back to the 1800s, became a strong influence in Europe in the 1920s, and continued to grow during World War II and after. Existentialist philosophy is characterized by works that express anxiety, alienation, and often hopelessness.

Soon after World War I, many intellectuals, writers, and young people became involved in a philosophical movement called Existentialism. Existentialists are mainly interested in the nature and problems of human existence. In this they differ from the traditional philosophers of Europe who believed that philosophy, like a science, is built around facts that can be definitely ascertained and that are always true. Existentialists, however, believe that philosophy is more like an art than like a science. They examine knowledge gained from the experience of the individual human being living in the actual world. The world is perceived as irrational and chaotic.

The beginnings of Existentialism go back to the 1800s, to the work and thought of the philosophers, Soren Kierkegaard, a Dane; Friedrich Nietzsche, a German; and the Russian novelist Feodor Dostoevski. Gabriel Marcel introduced Kierkegaard's writings to France in 1925. A little later, the German philosopher Martin Heidegger published his work *Being and Time,* which presents ways of examining human existence. Heidegger's work and the writings of Karl Jaspers, also a German, greatly influenced the development of Existentialism in Europe, especially in France. During and following World War II the movement became increasingly popular.

Jean-Paul Sartre was the French philosopher and writer whose works set forth an organized system of Existentialism. The writer Albert Camus, though not a philosopher, was closely associated with the movement. His novels, such as *The Stranger* and *The Plague,* helped make Existentialism part of the general current of ideas.

Many existentialists are not Christian and some are athiests. Some existentialists believe that even if there is a God, he does not give meaning to human life. These non-Christian and atheistic existentialists deny that there is an already-existing system of values, such as that expressed in the Ten Commandments. They believe that no matter how painful it is, each individual must accept the responsibility of establishing his or her own value system and acting in accordance with it. But Christian existentialists believe that a human being can build a personal set of values in harmony with God's purpose and give full assent to them.

All existentialists—believers and non-believers—speak of the anxiety of people in today's world. This anxiety became particularly intense after World War II (after 1945). Millions of Europeans had personally experienced the horrors and terrible destruction of war. That experience together with the explosion of the atomic bomb made many feel that the world they knew was ending. Young people no longer had the Christian faith and felt lost. The world seemed to be without ideals or values, and selfish economic interests ruled. Many people, no matter how much they wanted to feel that life was worthwhile, felt that they faced a vast emptiness. Nothing gave purpose to human life, except perhaps the routine of work. Individual human beings felt alone and helpless, strangers to each other. Death cast an inescapable shadow over each person's existence. Life was absurd and futile, existentialists believed. As a result, feelings of separateness or "alienation," of anxiety and dread were always present.

The existentialist movement included thinkers and writers of many countries. According to their different frame of mind they expressed different attitudes toward the problems of estrangement and absurdity. Some existentialists, like Sartre, found an answer in social responsibility and in an intense personal commitment *("engagement"),* often a political one. Others found comfort within themselves in the very keenness of their awareness and in the firmness of their decision to meet the absurd, if not head on, at least with grim composure. Still others felt logically driven to violent and desperate acts, even to taking their own lives.

Many Christians did not realize immediately that Existentialism was enriching philosophy with new data about human existence. It was raising important questions not only about private inner "worlds" of human beings but about their civil responsibility. Eventually, however, artists and theologians of the Judaeo-Christian tradition began to express in a new way the value of the individual person, the primacy of conscience, and the importance of freedom and authenticity in decision-making. Among these theologians are Martin Buber, a Jewish philospher; Rudolf Bultmann and Paul Tillich, both Protestants. The plays and other writings of the Christian philosopher Gabriel Marcel leave us with a clearer vision of the value of our life as we live it here and now.

The spirit of Existentialism came late to North America and England. Twentieth-century disillusionment with capitalism and a growing awareness of social evils were the soil in which European Existentialism struck new roots in America. Alienation in families, between generations, and in society became the subject matter of writers like Edward Albee, J.D. Salinger and Saul Bellow. The name "existentialist," however, is not widely used in America.

24. After World War II, many people thought of Europe and the world as divided into the Communist bloc and the Western bloc.

The peace which returned to the world in 1945 was a peace filled with tension and ideological conflict, all the more dangerous since more powerful and effective weapons of destruction had been invented. In 1945 the leaders of the major victorious nations, Stalin of the Soviet Union, Churchill of the United Kingdom, and Roosevelt of the United States, met at Yalta to consider the future. Their decisions affected the destinies of many nations and led to the division of Europe into two blocs.

In 1945 the United Nations was established in San Francisco. This organization brought together representatives of the majority of governments to solve international problems. Its specialized agencies dealt with economic and technical problems. Nations hesitated to give to the United Nations the power necessary to guarantee peace. Nevertheless, during the following decades, the United Nations helped keep peace in many areas, including Israel, the Congo, Cyprus, and Kashmir.

Between 1948 and 1951 the United States through its Marshall Plan offered extensive help for the rebuilding of Europe, where the destructive force of the war had been greatest. The leader of this effort, General George Marshall (1880-1959) received the Nobel Peace Prize in 1953.

From 1945 to 1960 the world seemed to be divided into two blocs. One included the Soviet Union, the dominant power, along with

China, North Korea, North Vietnam, and the countries of central and eastern Europe which had been awarded to the Soviets at Yalta. A special case was Yugoslavia, where Tito, the Communist dictator, had led the fight for liberation from Nazi occupation. Tito wanted Yugoslavia to be a Communist nation, but also to be independent from Stalin. So in 1948 Yugoslavia withdrew from its alliance with the Soviet Union.

The Western bloc, under the leadership of the United States, brought together western Europe, Canada, Turkey, Australia, and a few Asian countries. The Atlantic Treaty and the North Atlantic Treaty Organization (NATO) helped give America predominance over much of Europe. The European border between nations of the two blocs, which seemed to imprison those under Soviet control, was called the Iron Curtain.

Because relations between the two blocs were extremely icy and tense, the postwar period came to be known as "the cold war." In Korea, between 1950 and 1953, the conflict turned into open warfare. Otherwise, it took the form of a headlong arms race, competition to increase production, and rivalry to control sources of energy and raw materials. In the United States for a few years some persons, led by Senator Joseph McCarthy, blamed all troubles on American Communists and tried to purge supposed Communists from places of power and influence.

While Europe and America saw the world as two blocs, most nations of the world did not want to become part of this battle between the West and Communism. These nations of Latin America, Africa, and Asia were more concerned with freeing themselves from colonial political and economic domination and from poverty and hunger. This group of nations is often called the Third World.

25. In India, a great religious figure and symbol of peace, Gandhi, led a nonviolent struggle against British rule. In 1947, India became independent from Britain.

The greatest religious figure in modern India was Mohandas Gandhi (1869-1948). Gandhi was a Hindu, a follower of the main traditional religion of India. By 1915 he had founded his first ashram, a place where people gathered to pray, learn, and help the needy. Gandhi opposed India's caste system, which degraded countless people. Because of this system, most persons spent all their lives in the class into which they had been born. Some classes were considered very low and were treated as inferiors. Another major problem in India was the burden of being ruled by a foreign nation, Britain. Gandhi, known as Mahatma or the "great soul," led a massive movement of nonviolent resistance to the British authorities, who managed industry, agriculture, communications, and every other sector of economic and civil life. Gandhi called his method, which combined courage, nonviolence, and truth, "satyagraha."

Gandhi prayed and fasted and invited others to do the same. He encouraged peaceful strikes and acts of passive resistance. Indians stopped work, burned British products, and blocked trains. Gandhi was arrested repeatedly, but even in prison he continued to lead the great national movement. In 1931 he went to Europe to bring the misery of his country to the attention of the whole world.

In 1935 Britain was forced to grant India its first constitution. It was the first step toward independence, which came in 1947, after World War II. At that time many countries in the Third World were still controlled by European colonial powers. After India, many other nations of Asia and Africa gained their political independence.

Fighting among Indians of different religions led to a division into two nations: India, where most citizens were Hindus, and Pakistan, where the majority were Muslims. Later, Bangladesh split off from Pakistan.

Gandhi was assassinated by a fanatic in 1948. The Mahatma believed that the struggle for justice can be carried out by means of nonviolence. He appealed to the conscience and to the Christian tradition of the British people. Gandhi was attracted by Jesus but was repelled by the racism he experienced in Christian churches. For him, every act for justice and peace was related to the deep religious sense in human beings, and he believed that human beings in relationship with God were peaceful beings.

26. The World Council of Churches was formed in 1948 to promote contact among the many Christian churches and to work for greater unity. The Roman Catholic Church was not part of the Council, but it, too, began to work actively for ecumenism. In Taizé an ecumenical center arose that attracted young people from all over the world.

One of the most important new facts of Christianity in the twentieth century is the ecumenical movement, the movement of churches toward unity. The strongest push toward unity came from younger churches, formerly called mission churches. Differences in church government and worship and theology, which European and American missionaries brought with them, made little sense to Africans or Indians or Chinese. In fact, the divisions among Christians seemed to contradict the gospel, which claimed that Christ had broken barriers and reconciled people to God and one another.

The idea of forming a World Council of Churches, in the air before World War II, took concrete shape in Amsterdam in 1948. The assembly was attended by representatives of some 147 Protestant and Orthodox churches from forty-seven countries. The theme for discussion was "Man's Disorder and God's Design." There were heated discussions, but one thing was agreed upon: The goal of the assembly was not to establish a super-church with the authority to control individual churches, but to create a voluntary community of different churches. Like the United Nations, the World Council had to wrestle continually with the question of the balance between the newer churches from Third World countries and older churches from Europe and America.

While Roman Catholic leaders keenly felt the tragedy of Christian division, only in recent years did the Catholic Church officially reach out to other Christian groups. But preparing the way were many informal meetings for dialogue and prayer between Catholic and Protestant lay people and theologians. In 1960 John XXIII established the Secretariat for the Promotion of Christian Unity, headed by Cardinal Augustine Bea.

Another first took place in 1961, when a delegation of Roman Catholics, in the capacity of observers, took part in the general assembly of the World Council of Churches in New Delhi. However, it was the Second Vatican Council that opened a new era in Catholic ecumenism by urging Catholics to recognize and discover authentic Christian faith and values present among persons of other churches.

One example of different communions joining together to follow Christ was the monastic community of Taizé, France, founded in 1940 by Friar Roger Schutz. It was composed of more than seventy members from different Christian churches. One outstanding figure in it was Max Thurian, a theologian. From the 1960s on, many groups of young people from all over the world gathered on the hillside of Taizé and took part in the prayer life of the community. It was a visible sign of a new spirit spreading among Christians.

Less dramatic, but even more important, was the new spirit in parishes around the world, in city and town and countryside, as Christians of different traditions came together to pray, study, worship and work for justice.

27. A number of European Roman Catholic theologians expressed in their work new ways of relating theology to the modern world. Prominent theologians during the war years and after include Henri de Lubac, Edward Schillebeeckx, and Yves Congar.

Even before World War II, efforts were made in various nations to put theology more in touch with the modern world. Some Roman Catholic theologians wished to view the study of dogma and doctrine in a more lively way than the rigidly scientific approach of the past. They wanted theology to relate more to modern thought. The work of many of these theologians helped prepare for the Vatican Council held in 1965.

The work of Father Henri de Lubac is a good representative of these new trends in theology. He envisioned a general framework of theology which would bring together the modern findings of history, philosophical reflection, liturgy, and study of the Fathers of the Church.

During the years of World War II, Father de Lubac was a member of the French resistance. He had to do his writing while on the run from the Gestapo, the German secret police.

Many of his views were published in *Christian Sources (Sources Chretienne)* (1942 and after). This important work makes the ancient writings of philosophy and faith available to today's people. De Lubac also published an important work entitled *Catholicism* (1950). In this book, he gives a sacramental view of the Church. This means that he sees the Church, like a sacrament, to be both a natural sign and a supernatural reality. Besides being a visible society, with organization and officials, the Church is also, de Lubac stated, the means of union with God through Christ.

De Lubac focused attention on two extremes: at one end, the natural desire of human beings to "see God;" and at the other, the supernatural, which is God's gift to people. Some people thought that Father de Lubac stressed the natural desire to see God at the expense of the supernatural. He was criticized for "naturalizing" Christian faith.

Later, de Lubac's contribution to the Church was recognized, and in 1965 he was called to Rome to take part in the Vatican Council as an expert *(peritus)*.

Edward Schillebeeckx, a Dutch theologian, also expressed a sacramental view of the Church in his book *Christ the Sacrament of Encounter with God* (published in English in 1963). Schillebeeckx states that since God is totally spiritual and human beings are bodily creatures, contact (encounter) is not possible except through Christ. Christ is God's sacrament, by which he contacts people, and the Church is Christ's sacrament, by which people can encounter Christ.

One of the most important influences in preparing for the Second Vatican Council was the work of Yves Congar. Father Congar specialized in studying the Church, and in a series of books (1937-1961) he presented several ideas later utilized to varying degrees by the Council. Among them were these concepts: that the People of God—lay people—are called to full participation in the mission of the Church; that the Church is more than the Roman Catholic Church alone; that the mission of the Church is to be a minority in the service of the world. Congar also reminded believers that the Church is always in need of reform.

28. In an effort to bring the Church and working people closer together, the Catholic Church in France began the worker-priest movement in 1944. Some priests were allowed to work in factories, sharing the hard lives of laborers. But the experiment was ended after ten years.

During the first half of the century, the Roman Catholic Church in Europe realized more and more that the world of workers had moved far away from it. The industrial cities, with their huge factories, had created living conditions in which people felt ever more weary and alone. The Church and the parish did not seem close to them. What was needed, many religious leaders felt, were new forms of the apostolate to make clear that the message of Christ is for everyone.

Beginning in 1944, Cardinal Suhard of Paris gave some priests permission to work in factories, so that they might share the lives of workers. These worker-priests did not wear their clerical garb, but lived and dressed like the workers.

The experiment spoke to a real need, but it was ended by the pope in 1954 because of its upsetting effects on priestly life. When worker-priests found themselves face to face with the harsh life in factories, they wanted to make changes in working conditions. This led many of them into substituting economic and political goals for strictly religious goals. Some of the priests became Communists and some turned away from their former Christian faith. Moreover, worker-priests were isolated from their former life and often felt very lonely. The tension was too much for some worker-priests, and they left the priesthood. These were some of the factors that led to the decision to end the experiment.

In the United States and Canada, there was no similar worker-priest experiment. Many North American priests have been involved with labor unions and organizations as consultants and spiritual advisors, but not as workers. Also, in the United States and Canada, workers were not as alienated from the Church as were European workers.

The worker-priest movement has had positive results. One example is the story of the Dominican, Father Jacques Loew. A lawyer before he became a Dominican, Father Loew went to Marseilles, a port in France, to study economic conditions. He decided to learn more about the people of this port city. He got the necessary permission and papers, put on work clothes instead of the Dominican habit, and got a job as a dock worker. Loew was not used to manual labor, and his first days were very hard. Unloading freight from the ships, however, he soon understood why his fellow workers—Italians, Spaniards, North Africans—who were alone and weary in a foreign city, were giving up the religion which they probably had observed faithfully in their native villages. One day Loew glanced into a crate of fruit that he had to carry on his shoulders. He thought to himself: "It is something like the fruit in this crate. They need a community which is not so big that it will crush them but is varied and compact enough to keep them from being lonely."

Loew gradually created such a group. It became the Worker Mission of Saints Peter and Paul. Its members live the gospel message and share the condition of workers at the same time. They want to bear witness to Christ in the midst of workers. The initial group grew, and then a similar experiment was attempted in Brazil.

In 1968-1969 Jacques Loew founded the School of Faith in Switzerland. Its aim was to enable Christians to rediscover the certain truths of the Christian life and to live them in any and every situation.

29. After the end of the war in 1945, Pope Pius XII was able to turn his attention back to the life of his Church.
His teachings and his reforms are still important in the Catholic Church today. He urged active participation at Mass and frequent Communion. Also, he authorized a new form of religious life, called "secular institutes," for people who remained living in the world though bound by religious vows.

The end of World War II marked a turning point in the pontificate of Pius XII. He could now devote all his attention to the Roman Catholic Church and guide it in the difficult years of reconstruction. Pius XII gave strong leadership to the Catholic Church in a great variety of fields. From 1944 on, he acted as his own secretary of state, and gathered and kept to himself many responsibilities that popes had usually shared with their cardinals. Toward the end of his life, Pius XII had only a few close advisors. Thus the Catholic Church suffered from excessive centralization. That is, decision-making power was centralized in a very small group of people.

Nevertheless, Pius XII was a great influence for good. Ordinary pilgrims and travelers to Rome, convention delegates, and members of many professions and crafts (including doctors, lawyers, scientists, manufacturers, builders) came to listen to this pope. They admired his sound training and preparation, his tough perseverance in the resistance during the war and his clear thinking. The pope spoke to them about human dignity, the formation of conscience, and problems in professional ethics. In all these areas, particularly in the area of professional ethics, he left behind a body of teaching that was ahead of its time to a large extent and that is still valid today.

But the activity of Pius XII was not limited to talks. He undertook reforms in many areas, and those reforms were accepted and carried further at Vatican II. His liturgical reforms were particularly important. In his encyclical on sacred liturgy *(Mediator Dei,* 1947), he adopted the basic concept of the Liturgical Movement and recommended the active participation of the Catholic faithful at Mass. Following a tendency already evident in the work of Pope Pius X at the start of the century, Pius XII also declared that frequent reception of Holy Communion was a desirable thing.

Another important innovation of Pope Pius XII was in the area of religious life. In 1947, he approved the establishment of secular institutes. Members of such institutes took religious vows but remained living in the world. This was a new effort to meet the needs of the times.

During the time of Pius XII, devotion to Mary grew considerably in the Roman Catholic Church. A crowning aspect of this devotion was the pope's proclamation of the dogma of the Assumption of Mary (1950). This dogma states that the body of Mary the mother of Jesus was taken into heaven after her death and there reunited with her soul. It is an article of faith for Roman Catholics.

Two themes from the life of Pope Pius XII are shown in the illustration with this chapter: his declaration about Mary, which is suggested by the small picture cards; and his support of frequent reception of Holy Communion.

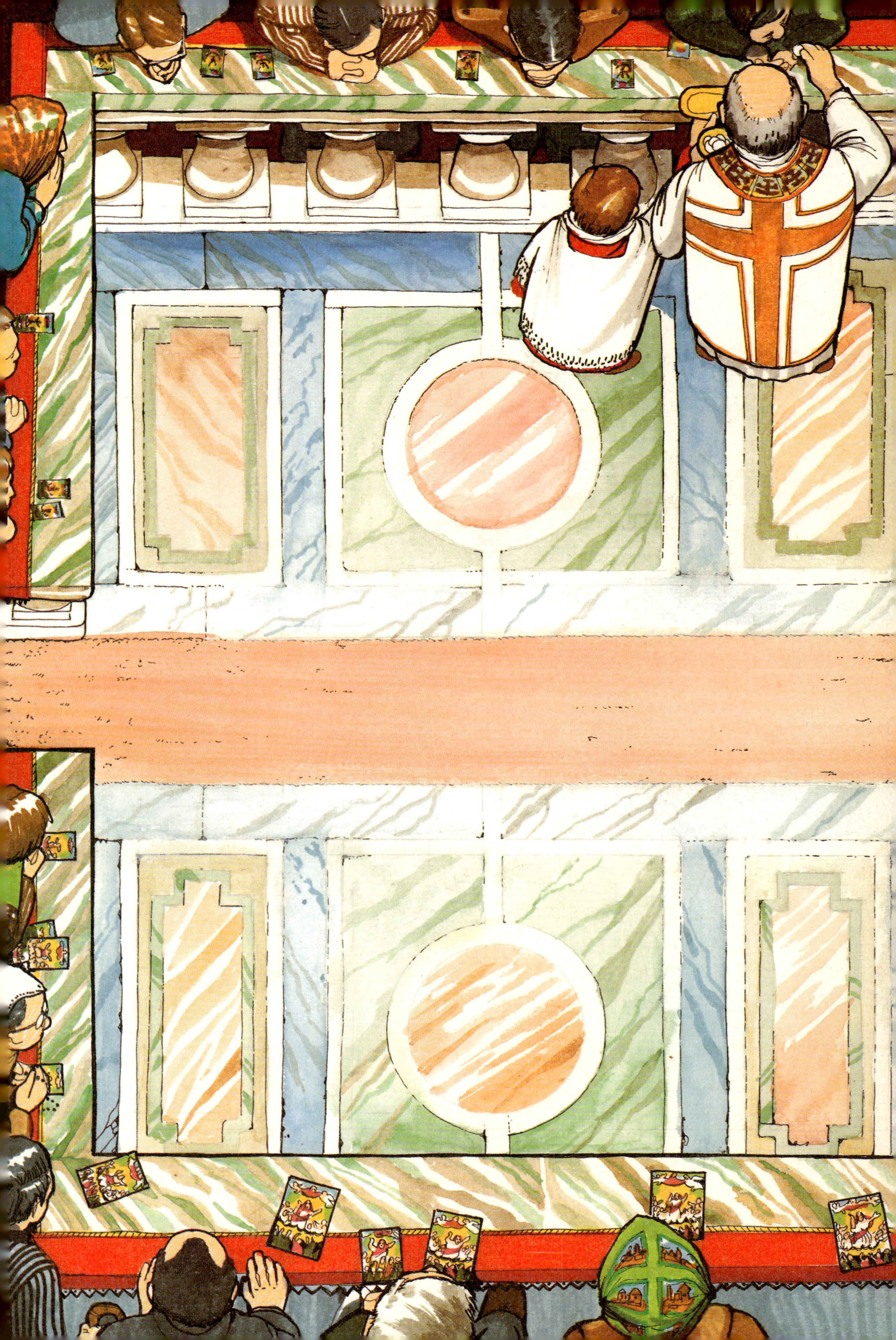

30. In the Communist controlled countries of Eastern Europe, the Church was persecuted with trials, arrests, and imprisonment during the years after World War II. Christians did not give up their faith, and the "Church of Silence" was born.

When Europe was divided after World War II, many Christians were put under the direct or indirect authority of the Soviet Union (Russia). They experienced terrible difficulties. The Soviet Union tried to repress religion and wanted to build a society in which God was not present. The Soviets enforced the same policy in the countries it now controlled. These countries included Hungary, Bulgaria, Rumania and Poland.

Some citizens in these countries agreed with the Soviets. Some of them were members of the Communist Party and had a materialistic and atheistic outlook. Also, many people of the middle class and many intellectuals had given up a religious view of life.

The hostility between the two blocs (Democratic and Communist) was another factor in the persecution. People in Communist countries who had friendly relations with people in democratic countries were regarded with mistrust and suspicion. This was all the more true of Catholics. The pope was considered to be on the side of the Western powers. Therefore, Communists looked on Roman Catholics as people who sided with the West against their own country.

For all these reasons, there was a wave of persecution against the Roman Catholic Church in the Communist countries during the 1950s. Many people were arrested secretly at night, and taken away to prison. When brought to trial, false charges would be alleged against them, testimony would be falsely sworn, and confessions obtained by torture. Soviet advisers helped judges and officials in the various countries to prepare and carry out these trials.

To strike down the hierarchy (higher clergy), the governments imprisoned bishops; including Beran in Czechoslovakia, Marton in Rumania, Wyszynski in Poland, Stepinac in Yugoslavia and Mindszenty in Hungary. They also refused to let vacant church posts be filled. Thus, many dioceses had no bishops.

Religious orders were viewed with special hostility. The religious way of life was regarded as a useless waste of energy and almost all religious orders were dissolved. Religious men and women were imprisoned, orders were forbidden to accept new novices, and were not allowed to pass on the religious life in any way.

Particular attention was paid to young people. Religious instruction was removed from the schools. Catechism could be taught only at specified times and in specified places. And, except for meeting at church services, young people could not meet as a religious organization. Publication of religious books and newspapers was forbidden. In general, all forms of Christian public expression were repressed.

If lay people were known Christians, they encountered countless difficulties at work, at home, and among their friends. Communist governments made it a policy to decrease the number of priests and to create a network of new priests loyal to the local government rather than to the pope. This system of "peace priests," as it was called, did not meet with much success, however. Many priests chose to be persecuted and even imprisoned rather than to accept the compromise. The Christian people also refused to place their trust in the priests who had made a pact with the Communist regime.

Despite all these measures and the violence with which they were carried out, the Church continued to exist amid these difficult conditions. It survived secretly in the woods, in city homes, and in the barracks of concentration camps. That is what church people mean when they talk about the "Church of Silence."

31. Teilhard de Chardin, priest and scientist, brought together Christian faith and the theory of evolution. His ideas on the movement of the universe toward unity in Christ have become well known.

On Easter Sunday, in 1955, Father Pierre Teilhard de Chardin died in New York City. At the time of his death, he was unknown to the general public but within five years his books began to be published and they were widely read. His ideas on the movement of the universe toward unity in Christ became well known and continued to be discussed and investigated in the years following.

Teilhard de Chardin was born in France in 1881. He became a Jesuit and was ordained a priest in 1911. Teilhard was deeply interested in science and became a paleontologist (a scientist who studies ancient forms of life). Teilhard went on several expeditions to China, where he took part in scientific excavations aimed at discovering remains of early people.

In the late 1920s, Teilhard was a member of a team of paleontologists working in some caves near Beijing when the remains of one of the early forms of *homo* (man) were dug up. This discovery was called Sinanthropus (Chinese man). It is also called the "Peking man." (Peking was the name by which Beijing was known in the West at the time the discovery was made).

Besides being a skilled, respected scientist, Teilhard was a Christian thinker. He believed that Christianity could respond to the ideas and use the knowledge of his time. Science is very important, Teilhard thought, but it sees "only the crust of things." He believed that we should not expect to get fundamental truths from science. Teilhard brought together Christian faith and the idea of evolution. His basic idea was that the entire universe is moving toward the same goal. He believed that for millions of years past, the universe, including our earth, has been achieving ever-greater organization and unity. Life developed, and then the highest stage of life, human beings. Life includes consciousness, or awareness of one's own existence. In people, consciousness includes the ability to think. We know, and we know that we know.

According to Teilhard, the movement toward unity did not stop with the appearance of people. Human life, he believed, through its ability to think, is evolving to higher and higher levels of unification and spirituality. Eventually, Teilhard believed, the development will become complete and will converge (come together) at a point he called the Omega Point. ("Omega," the last letter of the Greek alphabet, is often used to mean the end of a series.)

For Teilhard, this Omega Point was Christ. When the universe has reached the Omega Point, Teilhard believed, all will be united with the Risen Christ. This will be the Second Coming of Christ. Teilhard saw the history of the world as a movement toward Christ.

People who see this evolutionary development in the light of Christ commit themselves to taking part in activities that help the world move toward unity, and they give up desire for personal gain.

This explanation of Teilhard de Chardin's thoughts is only an introduction to his ideas. Since 1955, many of his books have been published and his theory is studied by individuals and groups. Undoubtedly, his work has influenced people's thoughts and will continue to do so for many years. And Teilhard's books have helped many people understand how to center their spiritual life more fully on the risen Jesus.

Nevertheless, during his life and after, Teilhard de Chardin's work was criticized by some Roman Catholics. In 1962, the Holy Office of the Roman Catholic Church issued an official warning about his theories.

Yet it is thought that Teilhard's theory was perhaps used by Roman Catholic bishops at the Vatican Council in the late 60s when they wrote the Pastoral Constitution on the Church in the Modern World. Many people feel that de Chardin's ideas show especially in paragraph 5, which says in part, "the human race has passed from a rather static concept of reality to a more dynamic, evolutionary one."

32. **Christians became more active in economic and political life. In the United States the election of John F. Kennedy marked the acceptance of Roman Catholics into the nation's political life.**

After World War II life seemed increasingly impersonal, particularly in the big cities. It seemed as if society were made up of partitions, with each human being inside a separate box. Indifference and barriers between people prevented them from noticing that some people were oppressing others. Some persons were rich and others were poor. Some persons were left on the margins of life because they were old, handicapped, or unable to work.

It was a violent society in need of greater justice. It seemed impossible for individual citizens to change things. More and more Roman Catholics in Europe came to feel they should participate actively in political parties and labor unions.

In both the nineteenth and twentieth centuries, Catholics in Europe debated about establishing Christian political parties. Some considered the effort a mistake because it tied Christians and the Church to one political tool. Others felt that Christians had to use the tools of modern society, like political parties, to defend the value of human beings and to obtain fairer policies with regard to schools, economics, social services, and individual liberties.

Italy and Germany, which had just emerged from fascist or Nazi rule, after World War II saw the rise of new and important Christian parties, the Christian Democrats. Adenauer in Germany, De Gasperi in Italy, and Schuman in France became leaders in this new political commitment of Catholics.

Catholics also approached the problems of workers. In Spain under Franco's rule, where voluntary unions were forbidden, Catholic Action groups of workers (HOAC) were active. These Christian communities of both workers and students sought to moderate the policy of the Franco regime and attain better conditions for workers. In other nations, where democratic government permitted voluntary labor unions, Christian unions fought to improve working conditions. In Belgium, for example, they sought to combat the harsh life faced by miners.

In the United States, John F. Kennedy in 1960 became the first Catholic to be elected president. Thirty-two years earlier, Al Smith had been a candidate for president, and he had faced bitter opposition because of his Catholic faith. Some Protestants had feared that a Catholic could not be completely loyal to America. Al Smith lost the election in 1928. After Kennedy's election in 1960, Catholics were clearly accepted as full Americans, and no longer simply as ethnic groups.

John Courtney Murray, an American theologian, helped American Catholics look at themselves in a new way. He stressed that the idea of human freedom and dignity was essentially Christian. Therefore, freedom of religion and other human rights should be supported by Catholics, not for the benefit of the Church but as a moral duty. He also fought hard for the rights of Catholic scholars to do their research and teaching without outside hindrance.

33. Hundreds of thousands of workers from southern countries were attracted to northern Europe and to the United States, where economic growth meant many jobs.

European businesses and industry had been severely damaged by the destruction of the war, but some countries and regions rebuilt more rapidly than others. This was particularly true of the continental and Atlantic regions of Europe. The growth of these economies meant greater circulation of wealth and an increased need for people as workers. The more industrial countries did not have enough workers to do menial jobs and the harder and more dangerous jobs in mining and in construction work.

Thus, during the fifties and sixties a large number of people moved from the south of Europe to the north; from southern Italy to northern Italy, Switzerland, Germany, Scandinavia, Belgium and Luxembourg; from Spain and Portugal to Germany, Belgium and England; from southern Yugoslavia to northern Yugoslavia, and especially to Austria and Germany, as well as across the ocean as far as the United States; and, a little bit later, from Turkey and the southern shores of the Mediterranean to continental Europe.

A similar movement affected the countries and regions south of the United States, such as Puerto Rico and Mexico. Workers in these countries headed north. In the United States, this influx was similar, but on a smaller scale, to the waves of immigration of the 1800s.

These immigrants left their native country, travelled in hardship, and after arrival, lived in poor housing and usually did arduous low-paid work. Even though they earned more than they could have in their home country, their lives were very difficult. Often, the men of the family immigrated alone, leaving their spouses and children behind to join them later, if ever. The immigrants rarely knew the language of the country where they were working, and they learned it with difficulty. Sometimes they were despised openly or quietly by the citizens of their new country.

In general, these immigrants came from rural areas where life was lived in close contact with the other inhabitants. Now they found themselves on the outskirts of big cities, working in big industrial concerns where each person was on his or her own and there was not much opportunity for people to communicate with each other. Moreover, in their native countries many of these immigrants were used to religion as a normal, openly shown part of life. In the new countries, the immigrant found that religion was quieter, without much visible, outward show. Hence, it became difficult for them and their families to continue in the faith of their parents and to educate their own children in it.

The European Churches were rather slow to take action to help these new citizens in their countries. The main initiatives were taken by Churches in their original homelands. These Churches established missions in the big cities of Switzerland, Germany and Belgium to help the immigrants.

The majority of the immigrants to the United States from southern countries in the 1950s were Catholic. Some brought priests with them. American bishops trained people to work among the immigrants, providing religious education for the children, and churches and centers for recreation and help for the adults.

34. **The Catholic school system in the United States reached a high point of development in the late 1950s, and began to decline after 1965. But the Catholic parochial school system is still very important in the educational life of the United States.**

Between the end of World War II (1945) and the 1970s, Catholic parochial schools in the United States went through a period of growth and then a decline. The Catholic school system had begun when public schools in the United States were strongly influenced by the Protestant religion. Roman Catholics objected, and they began to establish their own schools. These schools became especially important when thousands of Catholic immigrants came to the United States. Parish churches began to set up their own elementary schools, called parochial schools. By 1840, there were about 200 Catholic parochial schools in the United States.

In the mid-1800s, public schools in the United States became nonsectarian, which meant that no religious concepts were to be taught. But Protestant influence continued for many decades, and so Catholics continued to build their own schools. School-building was encouraged by their bishops who stated at the third Council of Baltimore in 1884 that every Catholic parish should, if possible, build a school.

The Catholic parochial school system

became the largest private school system in the world. In 1945, there were about 2,500,000 students in parochial schools, and enrollment increased so rapidly that schools became badly overcrowded. More schools were built during the fifties and early sixties in major cities and country hamlets all over the United States, but especially in western and midwestern states.

Besides the elementary schools, high schools were built, usually supported by several parishes or by the diocese. Private (non-parochial) high schools, often called academies, were established by religious orders. Catholic colleges and universities increased in number.

Beginning in about 1965, parochial schools in the United States began to decline. There were many reasons. Most often mentioned, perhaps, was the fact that the schools were not supported by public funds and the economic burden became harder and harder for Catholics to carry. Other reasons were just as important. In metropolitan areas, families began to move to the suburbs. The big inner-city parishes found themselves without enough school-age children to fill their schools. Moeover, in the first twenty years after World War II, there had been a baby boom in the United States as returning soldiers became fathers. But the birth rate began to decline after 1960, and as a result, school enrollments dropped too. Getting teachers was another problem. Catholic schools had relied heavily on religious brothers, sisters, and priests as teachers, usually at low wages. But after 1965, many religious orders no longer had enough members to staff the schools. Besides these factors, there was a growing conviction among many Catholics that parochial schools were no longer needed.

In 1981 there were 7,802 Catholic parochial high elementary schools in the United States, with 2,232,000 students. In that same year, there were 881 Catholic diocesan and parochial high schools, with 497,000 students. The system continues to be a very important part of the educational life in the United States and a very strong point for the Catholic Church.

- Countries independent before 1945
- Countries independent in 1980
- Countries with foreign governments in 1980

35. In the decade of the 1960s, almost all the African peoples north and south of the Sahara fought to win their freedom from colonial rule.

In the 1950s the activity of colonial peoples to win independence took on new vigor. Writers, politicians, and common people, more conscious of the importance of their own history and culture, defended their own dignity and united in the struggle for independence.

In 1952 a group of Egyptian officials under the leadership of Nasser undertook a policy of solidarity with other Arab countries. Libya was proclaimed independent in 1951, and in 1956 the French had to accept the independence of Morocco. In 1957 independence came to Tunisia. The Algerians, too, wanted independence; but also living in Algeria were many French people with strong economic interests and emotional ties with France. An all-out guerilla war began, ending with the victory of the Algerians in 1962.

The people and nations south of the Sahara also won their freedom from colonial rule. In 1957 Ghana became the first government in black Africa to win independence, under the leadership of Nkwame Nkrumah. Guinea followed the next year under the leadership of Sékou Touré. In 1960 many countries won independence, including Zaire, the former Belgian Congo. Others followed gradually. Only Portugal managed to hold on longer to its colonies of Angola and Mozambique, which became independent in 1976. Sometimes liberation was preceded by long years of political struggle, armed conflict, guerrilla warfare, and terrorism. Sometimes older tribal divisions were more important than the national boundaries drawn by European colonial powers.

The new governments were often shaky, economically weak, and politically insecure. Moreoever, Europeans, Americans, and in some countries Chinese and Russians continued to dominate the local economy, cultural life, and communications media. Economic and cultural independence did not follow political independence. Often African nations continued to grow crops to export to wealthier nations, but did not have food enough for themselves.

A major racial problem remained in the Republic of South Africa. A white minority which had lived there for many generations oppressed the black majority and imposed a regime of "apartheid," or strict racial segregation. In spite of these policies, the white-controlled government called South Africa a Christian nation. Protestant and Catholic missionaries helped to educate many Africans, and many African leaders were Christians. Nevertheless, some persons, both black and white, continued to think of Christianity as a white people's religion.

36. Many Christian churches organized charitable institutions to provide help for victims of World War II.

After World War II, millions of people all over Europe were in desperate need. Many of them lived in camps because their homes were destroyed or had been taken over by people of another country. They needed food, clothing, medicine, and places to live.

Christian churches all over the world responded to these needs, and international relief organizations were formed to help during the emergency. Many of these associations later became permanent private relief organizations.

In 1943, the Catholic Relief Services (CRS) was organized in the United States for the purpose of helping European refugees, without regard to race, nationality, or religion. Because the Roman Catholic Church was an international organization, it was well suited to be a channel for the distribution of help in other countries. Annually, it distributed tons of food (much of it supplied by the U.S. government) and clothing, and provided help of all kinds (including child care, nutrition, water supply) to needy people and disaster victims all over the world. CRS has helped hundreds of thousands of refugees to resettle in the United States and in other countries. In the 1980s, CRS was working in 85 nations, where it touched a hungry world of 18 million people.

Another important relief organization is *Caritas Internationalis* (International Charity). It offers aid during catastrophes, such as earthquakes, floods, and political upheavals. It also collaborates with nonreligious organizations, such as the Food and Agriculture Organization of the United Nations (FAO) which is concerned with feeding people; and with the United Nations' Children's Emergency Fund (UNICEF).

In 1945 the Lutheran Churches of the United States, through Lutheran World Relief (LWR), began to ship food and clothing to European war victims, many of whom were German and their former enemy. Lutherans in Sweden and Norway also provided important aid. In 1947 the Lutheran World Federation (LWF) established a refugee service that resettled over 100,000 Europeans who had been displaced by the war. Today Lutheran World Relief cooperates with other worldwide relief organizations to provide emergency and long-term help for people—especially in Asia, Africa, and Latin America. And Washington-based representatives of LWR seek to influence public policy in order to give the world's poor and hungry a better future.

The Protestant Episcopal Church is part of the Anglican communion and works internationally through the Anglican Consultative Union to provide emergency help for refugees and victims of disaster. During the 1930s, when it became apparent that victims of Nazism needed help, the Protestant Episcopal Church began to assist refugees. Today the Episcopal world relief organization works especially on the program of world hunger and also supplies funds to refugees, to help them develop their own resources.

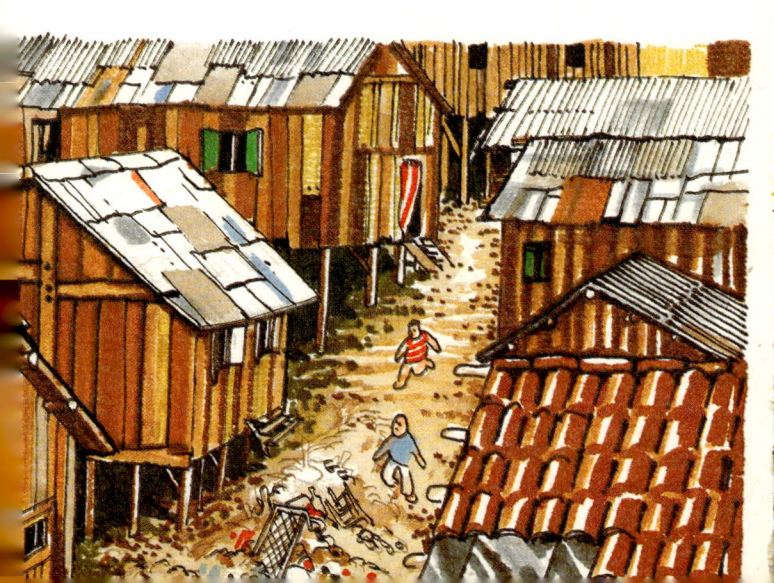

37. In 1958, a genial seventy-six-year-old cardinal became pope and took the name John XXIII. His plans for renewal were to change the course of the Roman Catholic Church

During the first half of the 20th century, rapid advances in standard of living, science, and education shook the world. Radio and, later, television and the airplane brought the human family closer together. The threat of possible nuclear war made it very clear that humans had to work together. As these things came to a head in the 1960s, a man of vision and hope appeared, a man who believed that the human family could face and overcome the challenges set before it. The man's name was Angelo Giuseppe Roncalli. We know him as Pope John XXIII (1881-1963).

Angelo Roncalli was the son of poor Italian peasants. After receiving an advanced degree in theology, Angelo was ordained a priest in 1904. He went back to his home province of Bergamo to serve as secretary to Bergamo's bishop and to teach Church history in the local seminary. In World War I, Father Roncalli was a chaplain at the front.

For almost forty years after the war, Roncalli worked for the Catholic Church in various official posts. During World War II, he was stationed in Turkey, as the pope's representative. The people there appreciated and admired his ecumenical spirit, his charity, and his courage as he worked to liberate German Jews from Nazi hands.

In 1953, at the age of 72, he became a cardinal and the patriarch (archbishop) of Venice. Finally, he could devote himself fully to the pastoral care of the faithful, the task for which he had yearned all his life. Venice, however, was not to be Roncalli's last home.

In 1958, Pope Pius XII died. When the college of cardinals met in conclave to choose a successor, they could not agree on a younger candidate. So they chose someone they thought would be a caretaker—that is, pope for only a short time. No one suspected the world-shaking notions which lay behind the broad smile and bright eyes of the new pope—Angelo Guiseppe Roncalli, Pope John XXIII.

Radio and television broadcast to the whole world the voice and image of the man who would soon be known as "good Pope John." Soon everyone would learn of Pope John's sincere, simple faith and warmhearted, open-minded temperament. People immediately sensed that the pope understood and shared their worries and concerns their hopes and joys. Breaking papal custom, John went to those in prison, visited the sick, mingled with the people on the streets with his heart on his sleeve. People responded to him with gratitude and delight. Both believers and nonbelievers showed their affection for this pope who so clearly demonstrated that, yes, popes were caring human beings, too.

In the late 1950s, during the years before John XXIII became pope, many Catholics recognized that the Roman Catholic Church had a great problem. The Catholic Church was an ancient institution and was proud of keeping itself unchanged. But how could it survive and continue its apostolate in a world that was undergoing such tremendous changes in society, politics, culture—in fact, in every part of its life.

Pope John XXIII began to show the way to solve this problem. Spurred on by his great love for others, he opened up a dialogue with the entire world. He even addressed his two encyclical letters, *Pacem in Terris* (Peace on Earth) and *Mater et Magistra* (Mother and Teacher) not just to his brother bishops but to all people of good will, urging everyone to work together for peace and human unity. Pope John expressed his openness by inviting the Catholic Church to open its windows to the modern world, to open its heart—as he had opened his—to the human community. This was Pope John's intent when he called for an ecumenical council.

38. The Second Vatican Council began in October, 1962. It brought together Roman Catholic bishops from all over the world. After several weeks of discussion, the bishops decided that the Council would devote itself to a study of the Church in itself and its relationship to the world.

When Angelo Roncalli left for the gathering of cardinals that would elect him pope, he said: "The Church is young." As pope, he strongly felt that the Catholic Church could and should open itself and learn more about the world in which it lived.

Pope John believed that the Church needed a true, inner renewal. It needed to ask, "What does God really want us to do? What is the best way to do it?" In January of 1959, he officially prepared for that renewal by calling for an Ecumenical Council of the whole Church.

The council came to be called the Second Vatican Council, or Vatican II. The Council opened in Rome on October 11, 1962. Its beginning session was a major event, reported by the world's press and media. In his opening address to the 2,540 Council Fathers (bishops), the pope told them not to listen to the doomsayers, and to take a positive view of the era in which the Church found itself. He urged the bishops to act as pastors, to work hard to bring people closer to tradition, and to do so in the most effective way possible. At the same time, he challenged the bishops to recognize and deal with the many changes that had taken place in society. He made it clear that the position of the Council was not to condemn errors or those who made them, but to clarify the meaning of church teaching so that all people could better know the truth and live out the truth in unity.

The Church had held 20 previous "ecumenical" councils. The first one was the Council of Nicea in A.D. 325, but Vatican II was the Church's first truly universal council, since bishops from all over the world attended. Vatican II also welcomed leaders of religious orders, "observers" from Protestant and Orthodox Churches, and a number of lay "auditors," both men and women. Theological experts *(periti)*, including John Courtney Murray, Henri de Lubac, and Karl Rahner, attended as consultants for the bishops. In addition, almost a thousand representatives of the world press and mass media attended.

Long before the opening session, however, many preparations were necessary. Ten preparatory commissions examined thousands of suggestions for debate, from bishops, theologians and leaders of religious orders. When the Council began, however, the bishops found that most of the proposals had to be reworked. The bishops wanted new ideas that would help them to be more effective and more in touch with the modern world.

Since the bishops did not know one another very well, they spent much of the Council's early days becoming better acquainted. Differing factions or parties did spring up among the bishops, supporting the various ideas being considered. Sometimes their debate, although respectful, became very fiery.

After almost two months of meeting the bishops were still uncertain what they wanted to accomplish. Then, on December 4, 1963, Cardinal Suenens of Belgium offered a direction to his fellow bishops. He suggested that they devote themselves to a study of the Church, not only as it was in itself, but also in its relationship to the world around it. To accomplish this, Cardinal Suenens, echoing the words of Pope John, called for an open dialogue (conversation) among the Catholic Church, other Christians, and the secular world. The bishops enthusiastically endorsed Suenens's proposal and Pope John supported it, too.

On December 8, 1962, the first session of the Council closed. Pope John promised to call the bishops together again. Although none of the major themes had been written up in a form ready for publication, the Council was well on its way. Before he could convene the Council for a second session, Pope John XXIII died, amid world-wide sadness. His successor would have to carry on the Council's work.

39. Paul VI succeeded John XXIII as pope. He continued the Council and allowed reporters to be present at Council sessions, thus furthering understanding between the Catholic Church and the world.

Pope John had set the opening of the second session of the Council for September, 1963. When Pope John suddenly died, the college of cardinals elected the Archbishop of Milan, Cardinal Giovanni Battista Montini, to succeed him as pontiff. The new pope took the name Paul VI.

Paul VI himself had been a member of the Vatican diplomatic corps and a co-worker with Pius XII. The new pope devoted particular attention to FUCI, the Italian Catholic Action organization concerned with university students. As Archbishop of Milan he was known for his active concern for social problems.

Soon after becoming pope, on June 23, 1963, Paul quickly made clear his intention to continue the Council. Using his diplomatic know-how, he prevented excessively fierce debates and established more efficient procedures. In his opening address at the second session he spelled out the Council's objectives more precisely: to define and renew the Church, to work toward unity among Christians (ecumenism), and to enter into dialogue with the modern world. The last issue was particularly dear to the new pope. Journalists had asked for better information. He was happy with the opportunity to provide this. He permitted members of the press to be present at the assembly's debates.

Pope Paul's openness greatly furthered understanding between the Church and the world. It later found expression in the Council's document, the pastoral constitution on *The Church in the Modern World.*

The Council would eventually issue 16 documents: 4 constitutions, 9 decrees and 3 declarations. Constitutions deal with the heart or meaning of the Church. They answer the question, "What is the Church?" Decrees and declarations deal with more practical questions and concerns. They answer the question, "How will the Church act?" Through these documents the Church strove to clarify its self-understanding and renew itself, to alter its attitudes toward non-Catholic Christians, to widen its perspective on its life and function, and to open itself to dialogue with all people of good will.

Pastoral Constitution on the Church in the Modern World

The joys and the hopes, the griefs and the anxieties of human beings of this age, especially those who are poor or afflicted in any way, are the joys and hopes, the griefs and anxieties of the followers of Christ; nothing genuinely human fails to find an echo in their hearts. …

40. Dramatic changes in the Roman Catholic Church resulted from Vatican II. In a series of documents called "constitutions," the Council called for changes in many areas, and especially in liturgy and Church self-awareness.

The most far-reaching findings and results of Vatican II came in areas where reflection and debate had been going on in the Catholic Church for some time. Two such areas were the liturgy and Church self-awareness.

In regard to worship, the constitution on *The Sacred Liturgy* originated from the long-active Liturgical Movement. The constitution stressed the necessity for "full conscious and active participation in liturgical celebrations" by the whole people. As a result, the Council Fathers called for Mass in the languages people spoke, rather than in Latin, and for greater attention to the scripture readings and the homilies or sermons which explain them.

The Council Fathers entrusted the task of making changes in forms of worship, such as the translation of texts or the turning of the altar towards the people (see the picture), to the bishops of each nation. The Council Fathers also called for the revision of all the sacramental rites such as baptism, confirmation and marriage, so that they might better "nourish, strengthen, and express" the faith for God's people. Most people regard the reform of the liturgy and sacramental rites as the Council's main purpose and its most radical revision. However, the dogmatic constitution of the Church is, in fact, the Council's most radical document and most important. This document, entitled *Lumen gentium* ("the light of nations"), explores the Church's understanding of its own nature and meaning.

It reaffirms and defines the Church as the living "body of Christ" or "people of God," with the mission to proclaim the gospel, to sanctify human beings, and to lead all to Christ.

Stressing the common priesthood of baptized persons, *Lumen gentium* envisions a Church of equality and unity. The documents say that those who make up the Church's hierarchy, deacons, priests, and bishops, and pope, hold office in order to serve the whole people of God. Thus, they have the authority to promote the unity and fellowship of the Church Christ calls to holiness. In keeping with the Roman Catholic traditions of veneration of Mary, the council related this holiness to Mary, Mother of the Church.

To demonstrate its changed attitude toward other Christians and Christian churches, the Council issued the decree on Ecumenism. Before Vatican II, the Church generally saw non-Catholic Christians as deserters of the true faith. In the Council's decree, however, the Church, for the first time acknowledged responsibility for the division between itself and the Protestant churches. Joining its voice with those of the Protestant World Council of Churches, the Council's decree called for reunion among all Christians and urged Catholics and Protestants to work toward this reunion through shared prayer, dialogue and joint action on social problems and concerns.

The dogmatic constitution on *Divine Revelation* recognized history's influence on the Church's life, faith and scripture. It encouraged an historical-critical approach to biblical research and declared that faith can never be static, but that the Church must continually grow in its understanding of the faith.

Finally, in the pastoral constitution on *The Church in the Modern World,* the Council broke with a centuries-long position of isolation from "secular" affairs. With this document the Council asserted the Church's willingness and need to talk with and to learn from modern secular movements.

As these documents show, Vatican II did much more than spend its time defining Church doctrine and dogma. It also gave new life to the dialogue going on within the Church itself and between the Church and the world. That dialogue continues to this day.

41. Pope Paul VI is remembered as the pope of Vatican II, because of his important work in leading and supporting the work of the Council after John XXIII died. He is also remembered as the first pope to make long trips to many parts of the world, including Asia, Africa, and the Americas.

Paul VI will probably be remembered in history as the Pope of Vatican II, because the Council was the most significant event of his pontificate (years as pontiff or pope). But a whole series of "firsts" gave his papacy a new and dynamic look. The pope wanted to bear witness that the Church in India, the United States, Africa, every country of the world, is the very same Church of Christ as that in Rome. By visiting these churches, the pope meant to offer encouragement to the Christians of Asia, Africa, and America, many of whom lived in difficult situations. In the picture on these pages, Paul VI is shown on his trip to India. He went there in December 1964, to take part in an International Eucharistic Congress held in Bombay. Television broadcast his trip and brought home to Christians everywhere the rich culture of the Indian nation.

Perhaps even more significant was the trip which brought the pope to speak before the general assembly of the United Nations in New York. This visit came at the time the bishops at Vatican II were discussing the relationship between the Church and today's world. In accepting the invitation to speak at the U.N., the pope wanted to stress that such a relationship is not only possible but also proper and necessary. The pope also pleaded for world peace, crying out, "Never again war!" He emphasized the duty of nations to strive for peace and pointed out that conflict always comes if one nation tries to exercise supremacy over another. Nations' true goal should be collaboration between peoples.

Paul VI also made an urgent appeal to eliminate the most serious injustices and the enormous lack of proportion between rich countries and poor countries. The same appeal was made by the pope in his encyclical on developing peoples *(Populorum progressio,* 1967), which became famous. Wrote the pope: "The hungry nations of the world cry out to the peoples blessed with abundance. And the Church, cut to the quick by this cry, asks each and every human being to hear his or her fellow human being's plea and answer it lovingly."

Paul VI, the Pope of Vatican II, died on August 6, 1978.

42. Most African nations became independent after World War II, and this helped Christian Churches increase their numbers in Africa.

In the exploration and colonization of newly-discovered lands by Western nations, there were often clashes between colonial governments and missionaries. The missionaries wanted to proclaim the message of Christ, rather than impose European rule. Often, they defended local cultures and human dignity in the face of colonial violence. That did not prevent colonialism from almost always succeeding in gaining control. This situation was true in Africa during the colonial era of the late 1800s and the first half of the 1900s.

The majority of African nations declared their independence after 1950, and this official birth of new states allowed the Christian Churches to act with more independence. As a result, the evangelization of the African continent in the second half of this century advanced greatly. Also, the Christian faith began to try to absorb African culture and society, rather than ask Africans to give up their own ways to become Christians.

Native churches now exist, and they work to help people improve spiritually and materially. From the standpoint of missions, the 1950s have been called the "African Decade."

In 1950 there were only two Roman Catholic African bishops. By the early sixties there were 22, and in 1972 there were 237 African bishops and 12 cardinals. One of them was Cardinal Gantin, who is shown here visiting a village. Today, African priests do social-welfare work as well as the work of evangelization. The African clergy take part in all sorts of activities, being present not only in the villages but also in the big cities and in ports. In these places, people need help from the Church in meeting and coping with new forms of social organization and work.

Of great importance, too, has been the training of young catechists (religion teachers). Africa is an immense continent. Besides huge cities, such as Lagos and Cairo, there are many small isolated villages, often far away from a priest. Helpers in the work of evangelization are needed, so the work of Christian proclamation has been entrusted to young catechists who have been trained by local or foreign clergy of their own area.

Yet, the Church in Africa is not without problems. Some new leaders are corrupt. Some African governments support the most powerful group in their country, no matter what its goals are, or they see in the Church's work a threat to their control of policies.

43. In the decade of the 1960s, a desire for change swept through the world. Cuba, China, and Czechoslovakia attracted worldwide attention. Many people hoped for liberation, but this hope often went unfulfilled.

In the 1960s many people truly became aware of the world as one place, where what happens on another continent is not really separate or remote. In this decade, people in many countries shared the conviction that a life with more justice and community among human beings was really close at hand. This conviction found inspiration in many places. Between 1957 and 1959 Fidel Castro (born 1927) and an Argentinian, Ernesto "Che" Guevara, led a successful guerrilla war in Cuba. They fought against a dictatorship that had the support of the United States. After this success, Castro developed close ties with the Soviet Union. Under Castro's rule, living standards were raised in Cuba, but dissent was not tolerated. In 1967 Guevara went to Bolivia hoping to arouse guerrilla bands throughout Latin America. He was killed the same year, but in Latin American nations guerrilla warfare continued for many years.

The Chinese People's Republic, led by Mao Zedong tried to change the most populous country in the world by Communist leadership in economic, political, and cultural decisions and strict planning like that of the Soviets. Many Third World nations watched China carefully, to see if Communism could provide a more comfortable life for persons in a poor country. Chinese nationalists, after losing China to Mao Zedong's Communists in 1949, controlled only Taiwan, an island off the coast of China. Taiwan developed close ties with the United States.

Another area of Asia that played an important role during the 1960s and 1970s was Vietnam, where Communist North Vietnamese fought the South Vietnamese. The north was supported by Russians and Chinese, while the south was supported by the United States. The war ended in 1975. It had been a tragic struggle, in which foreign actions increased the suffering of the country. Americans, both Christians and other, were deeply divided over their nation's support, and much of the opposition to America's participation had a religious basis.

In 1968 students in America and in various nations of Europe occupied buildings, demonstrated in the streets and called for changes in educational, economic, and political systems. Gradually, some workers joined them. The new atmosphere was felt within the Communist world as well. In 1968 there was a real change of government in Czechoslovakia. The new regime lasted only a few months, but while it lasted, the whole world saw a new image of Communism. Instead of brutal Stalinism, here was a more democratic Communism "with a human face."

The movement in the United States for better treatment of American blacks was part of this desire for change. This movement is discussed in chapter 45.

In many places the hoped-for changes have not come or did not last. Russian tanks ended freedom in Czechoslovakia. Most Latin Americans still are not free economically or politically. Castro has fallen under Soviet influence. And there has been a more secret, underlying defeat. Many persons who hoped to change the life of the world have since come to focus only on their own country, city, or social class. The fine human dreams of the sixties still await those who will make them real.

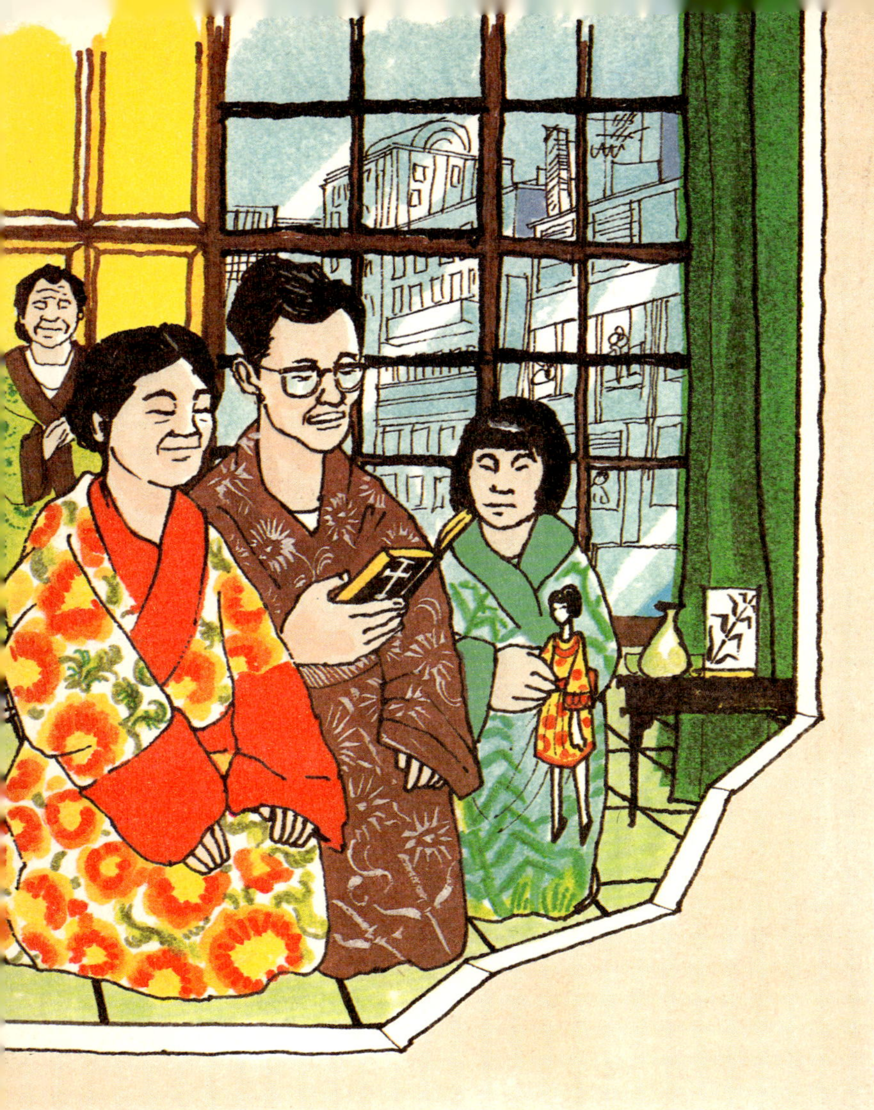

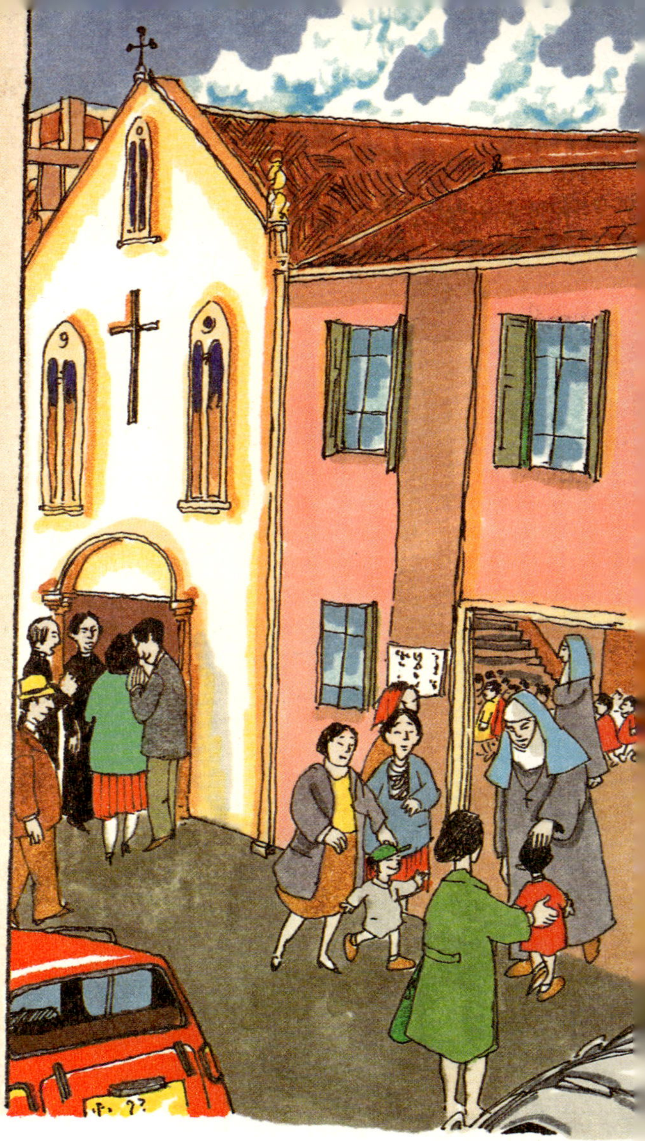

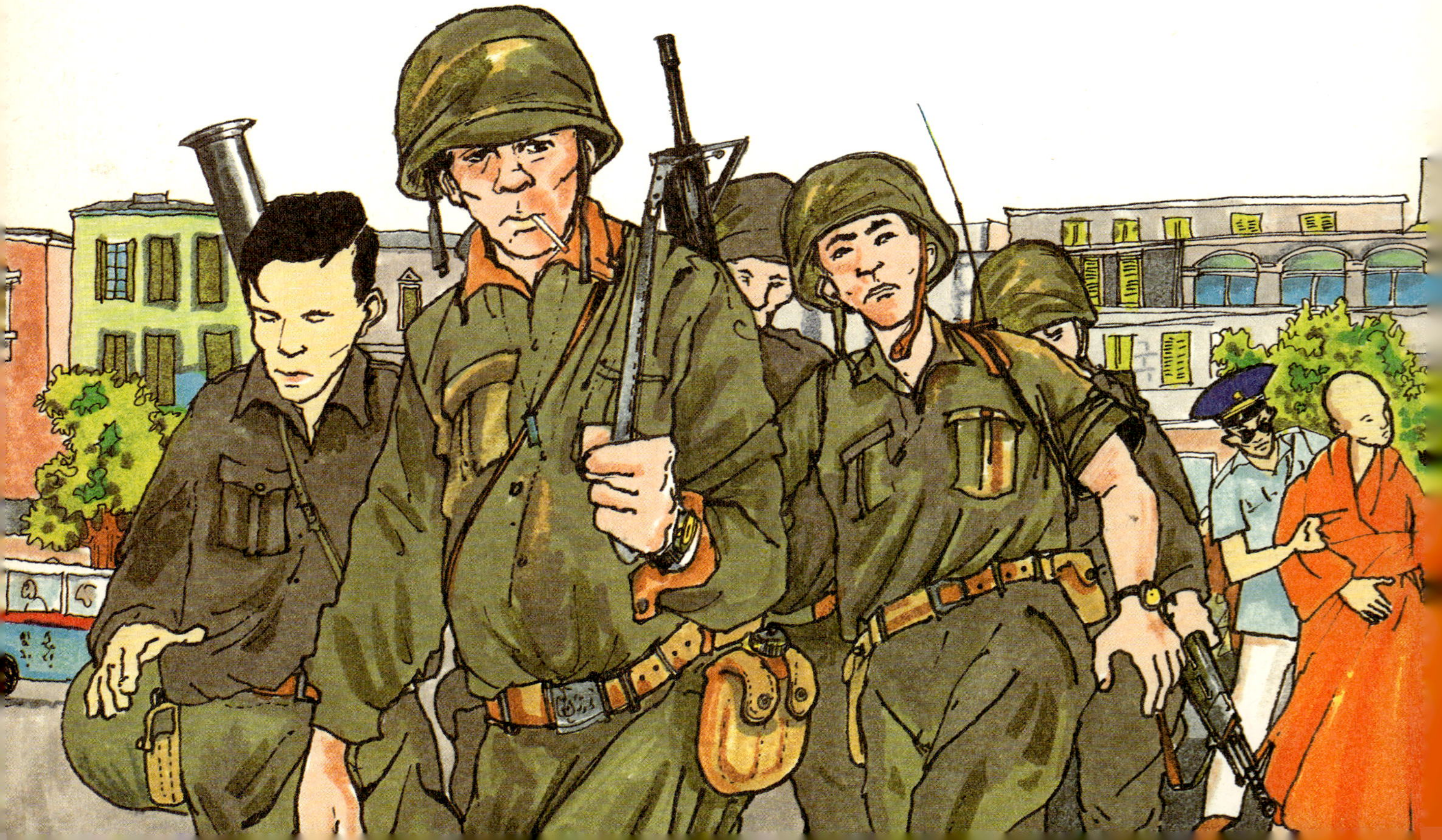

44. The Roman Catholic Church in the Far East showed new vitality in the 1960s and 1970s.

In the last few decades the Roman Catholic Church in the Far East showed new vitality. After passing through many difficult trials, it found new approaches toward renewal and service to the world.

In Japan the end of World War II brought a completely new situation. Shintoism ceased being an official national religion and became more a private one. Great missionary prospects opened for a short while. The number of new members increased, new schools opened, a Catholic hospital arose in Yolusuka. The number of missionaries increased, as did the number of Japanese priests and nuns. But Christians, both Catholic and Protestant, remained a very small percentage of the total population. Still the church exerted real influence on public life and had moral authority. No longer a group led by foreigners, the church spoke and acted as part of Japan. Japanese Christians had numerous opportunities to engage in dialogue with non-Christians and join with them in the service of human beings.

In North Korea, which was under a Communist regime, Churches in the west lost all trace of missionaries, bishops, priests, and lay people. It was uncertain whether there were still Christians there. South Korea was ruled by a dictatorship allied with the West. In the 1970s the Christian churches joined together in opposition of the government. Many persons suffered persecution and imprisonment. In the Philippines, the only Asian nation with a Christian majority, the Catholic Church has often found itself speaking for the poor in opposition to the military government.

In China, the Christian churches were harshly repressed after the establishment of the People's Republic in 1949. But faith was not erased. For years no one outside China was able to learn much about the life of the Chinese church. Later the West learned that there were bishops, priests, pastors, and lay people whose faith had endured.

In North Vietnam, the Catholic Church suffered from the opposition of the Communist regime. Missionaries were expelled, the activity of native priests was sharply limited, and the government tried to control the Church. In South Vietnam, too, the life of the Church was hit by the terrible conflict between North and South. Some missionaries and Vietnamese Catholics refused to support the government of South Vietnam. Many Christians and Buddhists saw the failings of the North and South regimes. They wanted peace and a new Vietnam, different from both South and North. This was not to be, and the victory of North Vietnam (1975) began a difficult period for the Church. Missionaries were expelled from South Vietnam and Vietnamese clergy were viewed with suspicion.

45. In the 1960s, a movement to secure the civil rights of black Americans spread throughout the United States, but was especially important in the southern states. Martin Luther King, Jr., a black Baptist minister, was a leader in this successful movement.

In the 1600s and 1700s many Africans were brought to America as slaves. Legal slavery ended in the United States in 1863, but most black people were still poor and badly treated. Throughout the country many whites unjustly treated blacks as inferior, but discrimination was most obvious in the southeastern states. There black people formed a larger proportion of the population; in some communities they were a majority. Black children usually attended separate, poorer schools. Most blacks were not allowed to vote. Black people often had to use separate and inferior restrooms and restaurants. In northern states, discrimination often kept black persons from living in "white" neighborhoods or holding better-paying jobs. Generally, Christians, even if they treated individual blacks well, did not challenge these expressions of societal racism.

Martin Luther King, Jr. (1929-1968), a black Baptist minister from Atlanta, Georgia, was the most prominent leader of the civil rights movements in the 1950s and 1960s. One example is his work to integrate the buses. In most southern states at that time, blacks had to sit in the rear seats of buses and give up their seats if white people needed them. In 1955, King led a successful black boycott of buses in Montgomery, Alabama, to end this practice. King led blacks in numerous nonviolent protests and appealed to the conscience and good will of whites. King also supported actions to help other minorities and the poor. In 1963 he led a peaceful march of over 200,000 persons, from all over the nation, in Washington, D.C. Partly as a result of this march, Congress passed laws on civil rights in 1964 and voting rights in 1965. King was assassinated in 1968.

Martin Luther King, Jr., was influenced by his Christian faith and by the example of Gandhi in India. Some Christians continued to support practices unfair to minorities. But King helped many Christians to see the conflict between racial discrimination and following Jesus. Many Christians, both lay persons and clergy, became involved in this struggle to improve America.

In crowded cities of America, especially in poorer neighborhoods, many persons never have contact with any Protestant or Catholic church. The churches which are there offer an appealing escape from troubles of prejudice, poor housing, unemployment, and bad schools. But they do little to try to change the world. In 1947 Don Benedict and Bill Webber, young Protestant ministers, started East Harlem Protestant Parish in a slum neighborhood of New York City. The area included Puerto Ricans, blacks, Italians, and other ethnic groups. The parish was supported by eight denominations.

East Harlem taught its leaders much about the church. Storefront churches made better contact than large, traditional churches. Small groups in which people worked, studied, and prayed together were essential. Members needed to be active politically to improve services. Persons were eager to hear good news about Jesus, but only from caring, trustworthy friends. East Harlem Parish is one of many attempts in recent years to bring the church closer to the impersonal life of the city.

46. Latin America, the largest area in the world that is almost entirely Christian, is also an area of great social unrest. Rapid growth in population has not kept pace with production of goods and services. As a result, there is great poverty, and in many Latin American nations the government is unresponsive to the needs of the people.

Latin America, from the Rio Grande River on the northern border of Mexico to Cape Horn, the southern tip of the South American continent, is the largest area in the world which is almost entirely Christian. It is also an area of great social unrest. The reasons for this are many. First of all, since the second World War the population of Latin America has been growing very rapidly, while production of goods and services has not kept pace. The result has been increasing poverty and misery for large numbers of people. The slums of Rio de Janeiro in Brazil and of Lima in Peru are among the most terrible in the world.

Also governments of the various countries have tended to be unresponsive to people's needs. These governments often reflect the interests of the upper classes or, sometimes, the interests of foreign investors. Almost all the governments of Latin America—Mexico and Venezuela are notable exceptions—have become military dictatorships which have failed to solve the countries' economic and social problems. Inflation in some places has risen to more than 100 per cent a year, and unemployment has been very high as well.

Under these circumstances it is not surprising that many revolutionary and terrorist movements have developed in Latin America. Governments have reacted brutally against any signs of dissent, and the violence on both sides has been savage. As usual in such crises, ordinary people have suffered most.

Nearly all Latin Americans are Roman Catholic, in name, at least, though many successful Protestant missions have been established in recent years. The situation for the Church has been extremely difficult, because Christianity must promote justice and also promote peace. The question in Latin America has been whether social justice denied to so many people can be attained without violence. Many Catholics, including priests and religious, have decided that the answer to the question is no. They have joined the revolutionary movements. They have also adopted what they call the "theology of liberation," by which they mean that it is a Christian duty to liberate people from political and economic oppression even, if necessary, by violent means.

In 1968, at Medellín, Colombia, opened the largest conference of bishops, clergy and laity ever held in the Latin American Church. The conference condemned revolutionary violence, but it condemned government violence, too, and it said that oppressed people had the right of legitimate self-defense. It urged that Latin American countries create social structures which would take into account the needs of the masses of the people. The conference also instructed the clergy to see themselves as apostles of social justice. When Pope John Paul II came to Mexico in 1980, he confirmed the decisions of Medellín and added that priests, while working for justice, should not do so by involving themselves directly in politics.

The Medellín Conference has had a large impact upon the conduct of the Church in Latin America. Even so, not all Catholics have agreed with its conclusions. The debate continues, and so does the violence.

47. As the constitutions of Vatican II were implemented, the Roman Catholic Church went through a crisis. The priesthood and religious life in general, the rites of the Mass and sacraments, and the way Catholics looked at themselves and their Church were all affected by the crisis.

Vatican II marked a turning point in the life of the Roman Catholic Church. Even before the end of the Council, many Catholics were becoming more involved in decision-making in the Church. National synods of bishops, priest senates, diocesan pastoral councils, and lay councils in individual parishes sprang up overnight. This concept of shared authority was not new in the history of the Church, but it was new to most twentieth-century Catholics. Many Catholics started to question Church authority. And as lay Catholics began to exercise more power in the Church, many of the clergy became less certain of their own particular place.

Priests have a sacramental ministry that cannot be exercised by the laity. Vatican II supported this, and also emphasized that all the faithful share, to some degree, in the priesthood of Christ. This new understanding diminished the priest's status in the minds of many Catholics, both clergy and laity. Also, some Catholics asked why women and married persons should not be priests. In the face of these changes and questions, many priests suffered great confusion about their proper role in the Church. Many priests left the ministry, and fewer men chose to study for the priesthood.

The crisis of identity also affected persons in religious orders of nuns and brothers. Before the Council, these people had been perceived by many Catholics as being uniquely different, often because of the special way each order dressed, lived in community, and practiced its spirituality. The Council documents caused religious orders to review their ministry in relation to the modern world, a review that often led to changes. Religious communities often split into factions which disagreed on the best way to answer the Council's summons. Thousands of men and women left the religious orders.

The reform in worship also brought about a crisis, not because the reforms were so radical, but because they were not radical enough. On the surface, most Catholics welcomed and accepted liturgical renewal, as the change in the rites of Mass and the sacraments is called. At a deeper level, however, many Catholics felt that something was wrong. The old rites of the Mass and sacraments had grown out of ancient social and cultural rites which were no longer part of modern life. But as religious rites, they were very familiar to millions of Catholics. Unfortunately, when the Church discarded these outmoded forms of worship, it unwittingly challenged many of their underlying religious meanings long held by Catholics.

The new rites, with the Mass in the people's language and the altar turned to the people, make the Mass knowable to people in a way that they could not know it before Vatican II. But, nevertheless, the new liturgical rites are still adaptations of religious models of the past. Often they do not reflect the religious experiences of people of today. Many Catholics believe that if changes in worship are to have a strong and good effect in the lives of Catholics today, leaders and pastors must listen to and tune in with the present religious experiences of the faithful. In the early 1980s, this is already happening.

Another question raised as a result of Vatican II concerned the governing authority in the Church. Some Catholics hoped that the bishops would have more power in their own country. Others wanted to diminish the traditional notion of papal leadership in the Roman Catholic Church. The Council documents, though they emphasize the importance of bishops' national and international synods and the teaching authority of the bishops, also reaffirm the dogma of papal infallibility and the pope's role as leader in the Roman Catholic Church.

The Council's call to the Church to enter into dialogue with the world has indeed led the Church into crisis, the world's crisis. And this has been a wise move both for the Church and for the world. For the Church, the "people of God" is firmly rooted and offers a vision of a redeemed and a redeemable world. The Church approaches the crisis with a wisdom refined by experience and a love fired by God. The Church and the world stand together in crisis, both poised on the threshold of change. And without change, growth is impossible.

48. As a result of Vatican II, theology was brought to the foreground in the Roman Catholic Church. Karl Rahner, Hans Urs von Balthasar, and Hans Küng are among the theologians of the mid-1900s who helped renew the Church's life.

Another result of Vatican II was to bring theology to the foreground in the Roman Catholic Church. Theology attempts to express in words our understanding and knowledge of God. Studies in theology go on continually because, as stated by von Balthasar, a theologian: "A truth which is only transmitted, without being deeply rethought, has lost its vital force." Thus, the work of the theologian is needed for the vitality of the Church. In chapter 27, we mentioned a few of the many theologians who paved the way for the Council with their writings, or who helped to deepen its documents and make them better known in the years after. Two other outstanding ones were the German theologian, Karl Rahner, and the Swiss theologian, Hans Urs von Balthasar.

Rahner was born in Freiburg, Germany, in 1904. As a young man he participated actively in the youth movement founded by Romano Guardini. He became a Jesuit and was ordained a priest in 1932. His teaching career as a theologian was interrupted by the Nazis. After the war, Rahner taught theology in the chief German universities. His reputation was so great that he was invited to Vatican II as a theological expert. Today, Rahner is generally considered the greatest Catholic theologian of our time. He has published a huge body of work. His central idea is what he called the "anthropological turn," the shift in attention to the human person as the object of theological study rather than God. In all creation, Rahner points out, the human person is the only being who relates to God. This relationship exists, Rahner believes, because God is already present in people, as well as existing around, beyond, and over all creation. Therefore, studying the human person involves studying God. And the study of God involves learning more about people. Thus, God acts in history through people. This is shown most clearly in Jesus Christ, the Son of God.

Very different is the thinking of another great theologian of our day: Hans Urs von Balthasar. He was born in Lucerne in 1905. Like Rahner, he became a Jesuit. Besides studying theology, Von Balthasar devoted himself to the study of literature, and this study had great influence on his own theological thinking. Von Balthasar maintains that the human ability to grasp beauty or glory is the best way to reach God. God manifests himself to human beings in glory, in his own proper splendor. Only people who are capable of opening their eyes and hearts to beauty are in a position to accept God's revelation. Von Balthasar says that glory, the free splendor of divine existence, enables us to comprehend God's love, which reached its highest point on the cross. We must respond with the same sort of love and unselfishness, and that may often lead us to follow the same way of the cross. Thus, the cross, transfigured in the glory of the resurrection, is the center of the Christian's life. Only in this way can the Christian encounter Christ.

Another important post-war theologian is Hans Küng who was for many years professor of theology at the University of Tübingen in Germany. Hans Küng became famous for his book *Council and Reunion* (1961) which made people aware that the Vatican Council II would provide many opportunities for reform and renewal. He is also well-known for his massive work entitled *On Being a Christian* (1976).

49. Russian exiles brought more knowledge of the Orthodox Church to the western world in the years following the Russian revolution of 1917. Also, there was a growing desire for unity among the Orthodox Patriarchs and between the Western and Eastern churches.

Around 1910, the Orthodox Church was expanding beyond its traditional strongholds in the Middle East, the Balkans and Central Europe. Many Orthodox Christians from those areas immigrated to Western Europe and North America. But the great wave of Orthodox migration was that of Russians after the revolution of 1917. Many of the people who left Russia were Orthodox, and they wanted to continue to live the Orthodox life. The Orthodox immigrants included many priests, excellent writers, top-notch intellectuals and theologians. They settled mainly in such places as New York, Prague (between the two world wars), and Paris. They worked intensely to establish themselves in their home. But they also worked with the enthusiasm of people who have a message to proclaim.

Such people as Berdyaev, Bulgakov, and Losski soon found an attentive audience among Westerners. They offered reflections on theology, history, spirituality, and ecclesiology (study of the Church) which had been worked out by the best Russian tradition. The institute of St. Sergius arose near Paris, and the seminary of St. Vladimir arose in New York. These Orthodox contributions came at a good time, when the richest strains of Roman Catholicism and Protestantism were seeking a less formal and legal concept of the Church. Western Christians searched for an act of faith more capable of rich union with God than they found in their current practice. They wanted a less secular vision of history than their own Western view.

The Orthodox proposed a vision of history as a salvation-happening, by picturing the community of believers as *sobernost* (a union created by the action of the Spirit), and by teaching the techniques of mysticism and heartfelt prayer.

Western interest in the Orthodox tradition led to the formation of various new organizations aimed at making the profound spiritual life of the Christian East better known. Among these organizations are the Dominicans of Istina (Paris) and the Benedictines of Chevetoagne.

The Orthodox Church had separated from the Roman Catholic Church in 1054 and the two churches had developed separately since then. Often, there were bitter feelings and angry words between the two branches of the Church. But in the 1900s, an ever-increasing desire for unity has been expressed by leaders in both churches.

In the Orthodox tradition there is no supremecy of one Church leader over the others, as there is in the Roman Catholic Church. Athenagoras, the patriarch of Istanbul-Constantinople, led the way in fostering dialogue and closer ties between the various Orthodox patriarchs, including the Russian patriarch. Thanks to Athenagoras' work, Istanbul-Constantinople again came to be a spiritual center and guide, as it had been in the golden age of Byzantium. Just as Athenagoras was concerned about Orthodox unity, so was he concerned about drawing closer to other churches. He established ties with the World Council of Churches and convinced other patriarchs to be more friendly towards Catholicism.

In Pope Paul VI he found an open-minded listener who was also looking for unity. On December 7, 1965, a joint declaration was read in Rome and Istanbul-Constantinople. The declaration abolished the judgments of excommunication which the two Churches had pronounced on each other in 1054. The way to a more fruitful relationship was opened once again and hopes for unity were expressed.

50. In Soviet Russia the Orthodox Church remains alive because of the faith of thousands of the Russian people. In self-published writings, called *samizdat,* Russians secretly share with each other their reflections about politics and the state of the world.

A few years after the death of Stalin, the Russian dictator, the Communist Party Congress of 1956 began to adopt policies that resulted in less oppression inside Russia. Also, Soviet Russia was more conciliatory towards the Western nations. This came to be known as the "thaw" in the "Cold War." The era began with Khrushchev and continued on and off up into the 1980s.

Living conditions for the Russians improved a little, and some expressions of religious belief were tolerated. But in Soviet Russia, individuals or groups who use their faith to understand and pass judgment on what is happening, or disagree with government policies, are often arrested. They may be sent to insane asylums, the Gulag (a network of prison camps), or into exile.

This whole experience has not been without benefit for the Church. Its life goes on in prison camps; in secret meetings between a few people; in spiritual exercises preached secretly in the woods; in the efforts of educated people and theologians to rethink the Christian faith; in the calm decisions of thousands of Christians to have their children baptized, to teach them how to pray, to keep churches open, and to continue processions and other public acts of faith. All these things have laid the groundwork for a future renewal of the Christian life in Russia.

Russian Christians, in spite of oppression, give public expression of their own experiences and beliefs. One way is through their contributing to a form of publication known as *samizdat*. As suggested by the picture, the word means "self-published." Samizdat publications are secret. They are done in people's spare time, at great personal risk. The tools are simple ones that might be found in the home: a typewriter and perhaps a mimeograph machine. Once produced, the pamphlets or manuscripts are passed from hand to hand in secret. But they arouse such interest that they sometimes reach the most desolate places. Writing for the publication is risky. In Soviet Russia, texts written by free people are seized, just as are the texts and correspondence of prisoners in jails or camps. Samizdat continues the Russian cultural tradition, since poetry and literature serve as ways of expressing one's personal reflections and conceptions of the world.

Christian believers are not the only people behind Russian samizdat, but they make important contributions. They pass clearcut judgment on what is going on and insist that the Russian people must return to the faith if they ever want to put an end to the world of the Gulag. Their judgment on the West is harsh too. According to many Russian believers in exile, such as the author, Solzhenitsyn, Western materialsm is paving the way for a barbarism like that of the Soviets. The only way to prevent this, they believe, is to return to a religious view of the world.

51. In Poland, Yugoslavia, Czechoslovakia, and the other Communist-dominated countries of Europe, the life of the Church continued under great difficulties during the 1960s and 1970s.

From the 1960s on, there have been more possibilities for church life in the people's republics (Communist-dominated countries) of continental Europe. This has been due partly to the desire of the government to quiet opposition within the nations and partly due to changes in Soviet policy. Russia exerts a strong influence on its satellite countries. The improvement does not mean that full peace has been reached. But the Church does have more bargaining power and more chances to carry on and express its life.

After 1960 the situation of the Roman Catholic Church in Yugoslavia definitely took on a more positive tone. In Yugoslavia in the 1980s there is catechetical work among young people, and involvement of lay people. Also, cultural and educational information is being spread. After a decade of being somewhat cut off from the rest of the world, Yugoslavian priests began to be informed of new thoughts and experiments in the worldwide Church. This work was begun back in the years of Vatican II by the periodical entitled *Glas Koncila* ("Voice of the Council").

In Czechoslovakia in the late 1960s, the life of the faith was continued, though with difficulty. Pastoral work among families and catechetics for young people was renewed, and some religious orders restored. Work for priestly renewal was led by such men as Anton Mandl who had managed to continue their priestly service while imprisoned in concentration camps.

In the late 1970s, difficulties returned for the Church in Czechoslovakia, to some extent. There was no total persecution of the Church, but attacks were made on the most important people.

From the late 1700s until 1919 Poland had been partitioned among Austria, Russia, and Germany. During those years, the Roman Catholic Church had been an important factor in enabling the Polish nation to continue to live, to renew its own language, and to develop its own culture. After World War II, Poland came under the domination of Russia. A decade of repression followed, and the situation began to change when strikes in the fall of 1956 gave power to moderate Communists. Cardinal Wyszynski, the primate (leading bishop) of Poland, and other imprisoned priests were freed. An agreement was reached between the papacy and the governing powers of Poland. Some opportunities for cultural expression and newspaper publication were granted.

Today in Poland, a great deal of Catholic activity continues. Numerous people attend church regularly and go on the traditional pilgrimage to the shrine of our Lady of Czestochowa. (This is the title under which Mary the Mother of Jesus is honored in Poland.) There is also intellectual activity in the big cities. This ferment of Catholic activity among the Polish people was one of the chief factors in the rise of the great unifying movement known today as Solidarity.

52. "The whole Church is missionary" describes missionary activity in the world today. Clergy and lay people of many various nations work together, each using the rich resources of their own culture.

Missionary activity in the Roman Catholic Church has decisively changed its look. As Paul VI said in his encyclical *On the Evangelization of the Modern World (Evangelii nuntiandi,* 1975): "The whole Church is missionary." That is, the Church in every part of the world is on a mission. And wherever the Church exists, it has a missionary apostolate to the people in its land.

as they seek to become fully self-sufficient. Lay volunteerism remains a way for many Christians to help. Such volunteer workers—often from other nations—carry out projects which the African Church wants to support but cannot for lack of money.

Besides being responsible for the life of the Catholic Church in their own nations, priests, bishops and cardinals from many different

For example, in Africa, the native clergy are becoming more and more important and more African men are studying to become priests. African bishops, native and foreign, have formed a continent-wide association in which they meet and plan together. The African churches seek to travel their own "African way," utilizing their native customs and music in their new faith.

African nations, like other developing nations, need economic, technological and scientific aid

countries of the world are taking positions of responsibility that have to do with all Christendom. And with today's advanced methods of communication and transportation, the local and national churches keep in close contact with the universal Church. This is shown in one of the pictures on this page, where we see priests and bishops of every country in the corridors of the Vatican, participating in the decision-making work of running the Catholic Church.

53. In a time of rapid change, such as the twentieth century, many people find all institutions and customs, including religious ones, inadequate. But some persons have found new life and vitality in their faith and in the Church through charismatic renewal. Lay participation and a deep sense of God's power today bring life to this movement.

All periods of history have experienced changes. Bur our era seems to revel in change for its own sake. We hope for something new that will give a different shape to our lives. As a result, in the second half of our century we have taken a close look at all our habits and customs—in family life, in work, in education. The same questioning has come to our churches and religious life.

Our desire as human beings to move out of ourselves, toward something that lies beyond, is part of being human. In this century of confusion, many activities have revealed the human yearning—however much disguised—for the sacred, for God. It is as if worship and other work of the churches had not provided enough food for the human hunger for God, as if it were necessary to make room for our religious impulses to operate.

One promising sign of this hunger in the church is the charismatic (from "charis," the New Testament Greek word for a gift from God) or pentecostal movement. (Pentecostal comes from Pentecost, the day of the beginning of the missionary growth of the church, as told in Acts 2). Special awareness of the Holy Spirit and the gifts of the Spirit marked the early church. Many Christians today think of the Spirit as limited to work not seen or felt directly by the believer. While many Christians stress the authority of tradition and the Bible, Christians in the charismatic movement are looking for the ongoing, visible presence of the Holy Spirit today. The Spirit, they believe, continues to distribute gifts today, and we can experience them directly.

The pentecostal movement started among Protestants in the United States in the late 1800s and led to the start of several new denominations. In the 1960s this movement came to the Roman Catholic Church and to major Protestant denominations, such as Lutheran, Episcopal, and Methodist. Charismastics claim to have a fresh experience of the Holy Spirit which is promised in baptism, the gift of speaking in tongues (praising God in sounds not from any known language), and, often, a gift of healing. Persons find an exciting contrast to the seeming apathy or routine of their previous life in churches. Informality and stress on individual experience and feelings give many a sense of importance they do not feel in traditional worship. Some charismatic persons have formed communities which live together or meet frequently for worship and social contact.

In the Catholic Church, this movement, called charismatic renewal, began in 1967 at Duquesne University in Pittsburgh and soon spread to Notre Dame and elsewhere. Priests, nuns, and lay persons found new spiritual life in meeting for prayer and sharing in homes, on campuses, in churches. Pentecostalism among Roman Catholics has not been limited to the United States. Cardinal Suenens of Belgium, a progressive leader at Vatican II, identified himself with the movement. Paul VI, while not a charismatic, expressed support as he blessed a group of 10,000 charismatic Catholics who were on a pilgrimage to Rome in 1975.

Many charismatics seem to have a faith rooted only in emotion and are suspicious of learning and reason. Others focus on individual experience and neglect social concerns. Some give the impression of thinking of themselves as superior to other Christians.

However, in many ways the charismatic movement shares in the spirit of Vatican II. Lay persons and clergy pray and work together, with the barrier between them sometimes disappearing. Persons find a close relationship to other Christians. Many experience a fresh sense of the reality of God and the power of God's Spirit.

54. The twentieth century is an era of Christian movements which have had important influence on church and social life.

In this chapter and the next, a number of Christian movements are described which are especially significant in church and social life during the middle years of the twentieth century.

Bread for the World (BFW) is a Christian citizens' movement in the United States that brings together members of many religious faiths. Founded in 1973, Bread for the World is the only citizens' lobby on hunger issues. It has been instrumental in passing legislation that directly benefits the hungry both in the United States and around the world. Two notable examples are: In 1980, BFW aided in the passage of the Emergency Grain Reserve Act, which set aside four million tons of wheat for emergency food assistance. In 1981, BFW lobbied for the Hunger and Global Security Act, which was passed by the U.S. Congress. This act reformed United States foreign aid so that more foreign aid dollars were directed to the poorest of the poor in underdeveloped countries. BFW members lobby for their cause in various ways, including writing to their senators and representatives.

Another group that combines Christian beliefs with social action is the Sword of the Spirit, a movement inspired by Christopher Dawson and launched in 1940 by Barbara Ward (Lady Jackson). Its goal was to fight totalitarianism (dictatorships) and to unite people in efforts to secure a Christian peace. In 1942, the Church of England, the Church of Scotland, the Free Churches, and the Sword of the Spirit pledged to work jointly in the field of social and international ethics. Since 1950, the organization's chief work has been spreading information about aid to developing countries, the United Nations, and the concept of European unity.

The Grail, an international movement, was founded by Catholic laywomen of Holland in 1921. Today, the Grail is active in 24 countries and on all six continents, and its members are from each country it serves. Married, single, and celibate women from every walk of life make up the Grail. Together and singly, in Grail projects and in their professional and family lives, Grail women seek to bring to life the religious, social, political values most needed in their societies. Medical services, cultural programs, value-oriented education are among the specific methods, which vary with the needs of the different cultures. In the United States, the national headquarters is at Grailville, near Loveland, Ohio.

Two European-originated movements that have spread to the United States are the Cursillo and the Focolari movements. A cursillo is a three-day meeting where people meet, live, and study together. Afterwards they are encouraged to form small actively Christian groups in their own areas.

The Focolari creates spiritual families. It invites Christians to unite to help each other in their own locality and to encourage others to do the same. Its members, called focolarini, now number many thousands in more than thirty countries. Among other things, focolarini do important publishing work.

55. Various forms of the retreat movement emphasize that Christianity should be part of one's whole life.

In different parts of the world, a number of movements have arisen that emphasize that Christianity should not be confined to one's private life. One example of such a movement is Communion and Liberation, founded by Father Luigi Guissani in Italy in the 1960s. Communion and Liberation helps people realize that the Christian community can be created anywhere: in a university, a neighborhood, or a factory. Members of Communion and Liberation believe that Christianity should not be an island, separated from the rest of humanity. Instead, Christianity should help people enjoy and appreciate all the experiences of human beings and step in and help when needed.

In Poland, the Light and Life movement has helped thousands of young people find and experience the full humanness of Christianity amid a society ruled by a communist-dominated government. The movement, founded in Katowice by Father Flachnicki, centers around encounter weeks called "Oases," when people come together to recapture the spirit of Christian life. Young people from all over Poland attend these weeks.

In the United States, changes in the Roman Catholic retreat movement reflect the modern emphasis on full Christian living. Retreats were brought to the United States by religious orders and were originally attended only by priests and religious brothers and sisters. Later men were included, and in 1892 the Cenacle, an order of nuns, began giving religious retreats to lay women in their retreat houses.

Until the mid 1960s, Roman Catholic retreats always followed the same general plan: retreatants lived together in an atmosphere of silence for two or three days (sometimes longer), taking part in Mass and other religious devotions (such as the Rosary, the Way of the Cross), attending conferences (talks) on Christian living and the Catholic faith, and spending time in personal prayer and reflection.

The movement grew tremendously, but following Vatican Council II, people began asking for dialogue with retreats. Instead of only listening, they wanted to discuss the things they heard and ask questions. Also, they were hungry for more community building and spirit within retreats. As a result, retreats changed. Also, in the years of upheaval following Vatican II, other activities within and without the Church attracted many people who formerly had made an annual retreat. Attendance at retreats fell off.

But in the 1970s, interest in the spiritual life grew stronger and retreats became popular again. Today, Roman Catholic retreats take many forms. There are: dialogue weekends with discussion and open communication; home retreats; retreats in daily living; and, still, traditional retreats with conferences.

Retreats are becoming more and more popular in the Protestant Church of the mid-twentieth century. Among Lutherans in the United States, they are often conducted away from the church facilities, usually last from one to three days, and are designed for small groups. Some retreats serve specific needs, such as committee planning, Confirmation preparation, short courses on the Bible, church history, prayer—or on social issues, such as justice, hunger, war. Even in those retreats that are nondirective, the goal is always to provide opportunity for meditation, inspiration, and renewal. The chance for discussion and fellowship is always part of the retreat.

In these many forms, the retreat is for the sake of full Christian living in the world and in relationship with God, self, others, and the world itself.

56. Mother Teresa of Calcutta is an example of Christian dedication to the poorest of the poor. She was awarded the Nobel Peace Prize for her work. Another example is Jean Vanier, founder of Ark —a series of homes where mentally handicapped persons may live as part of the family.

The growth of the world's population aggravated problems of worldwide hunger and worldwide poverty in the mid and later 1900s. This situation demands the help of Christians. A courageous example in this field has been given by Mother Teresa of Calcutta, a nun who has spent her life caring for the poor and the sick in that large city of India.

Mother Teresa was born in 1910 in Skopje, a small town on the border between Albania and Yugoslavia. Her parents were merchants. They sent Agnes, as Mother Teresa was named before she became a nun, to the best schools in the area. At the age of 18 she surprised everyone by deciding to become a nun. She entered a missionary congregation. After her novitiate she was sent to Calcutta (India) to teach school. As the years passed, however, she found that this work did not satisfy her. It seemed foolish to her that she spent her time teaching a small group of well-to-do girls while so many people were dying of hunger around her. She asked her superiors for permission to leave the convent and work among the poor.

In 1948, Mother Teresa took off her nun's habit and donned the white *sari* worn by poor Indian women. She went to live in the shanties on the outskirts of Calcutta. She was given two rooms, which she quickly filled with sick people from off the streets.

Some of Mother Teresa's students came looking for her, bringing money and rice with them. This was fortunate because Mother Teresa welcomed all the needy and her work soon increased greatly. Abandoned newborn babies were cared for in rudimentary incubators; jobs were found for boys on the loose; dying people were picked up, taken to a hospital and washed so that they could at least die as human beings.

Starvation and poverty were not restricted to Calcutta, so Mother Teresa began to travel around. Wherever there was a need, she established a house, left behind a small group of her sisters (which gradually grew to over a thousand), and then set out in search of more poor people.

Help and recognition began to come to her. The most distinguished recognition and help was the Nobel Peace Prize, awarded to her in 1980.

Another significant example of Christian charity is that of Jean Vanier. Canadian by birth, he was a professor of philosophy in France. Every now and then he would go to a hospital to visit two children who were mentally handicapped. One day he suddenly felt that was not enough. He bought an old house near Compiègne, north of Paris, and there he lived with Raphael and Phillip. That was only the beginning, however. Soon other handicapped people began to arrive, and Jean Vanier did not want to build another hospital. He felt that the mentally handicapped needed human contact more than anything else, so he decided to offer them a family-like atmosphere. He needed many little houses and many assistants. With God's help he found both. Then there was the problem of work. Vanier set up various workshops because the handicapped, too, needed to express themselves through work. Vanier opened his first house, which he called "Ark," in 1964. Today there are more than fifty such houses to be found around the world.

57. Karol Wojtyla, a Pole, became Pope John Paul II in 1978, the first non-Italian pope in 600 years. From his background as a cardinal in a Communist-dominated country, he brought to the papacy important experience in dealing with hostile regimes. He also brought great personal charm and character to his office.

In August 1978, Pope John Paul became head of the Roman Catholic Church. He combined in his name the names of two preceding popes, Paul VI and John XXIII. John Paul died after only a month in office. He is remembered as the smiling pope because of his friendliness.

In October, 1978, Karol Wojtyla, a Pole, became pope. He was the first non-Italian pope in six hundred years. He, too, took the name John Paul.

As a young man during the German occupation of Poland, Karol Wojtyla had worked in a factory and had been an actor. He studied for the priesthood in secret seminary, and as a priest and bishop, he became known as a scholar, the author of many philosophical and poetic books, and a university teacher. In Cracow, Cardinal Wojtyla had gathered around him many of the most lively Polish thinkers.

Living in Poland under the Communist government had given him much experience in dealing with a hostile regime. Life with the Polish people and the cultural battle between

Poles and Communism were daily experiences for him. Polish bishops had never felt timid before the Communistic government. The people were with the Church, the bishops knew, not with the Communists.

When Cardinal Wojtyla became pope, he soon revealed to the world great charm and character. Probably his background as an actor helped him use television and other modern media to great advantage. In his addresses he directed himself to all human beings, not just to Christians. His predecessors had done this too, but John Paul II did it in a more noticeable and public way.

As he had usually spoken to the Poles, so he spoke to all: Jesus Christ came to save humanity, so all human beings should know that they have been created for a greater life now, right away.

In 1981, Pope John Paul II was wounded in an assassination attempt as he greeted crowds in St. Peter's Square. After several months of illness due to the wound and infection, he reached good health again.

John Paul II has traveled a great deal, and he has been greeted by huge crowds of people in Africa, North America, and Europe. Again there is a ruler in whom people can believe. Many non-Christians see a friend in this pope, who displays the humanity of Christianity in his person and his actions.

58. Peace, disarmament, genetics, pollution, poverty, and genocide are among the issues of the late twentieth century. Today, people are able to destroy life on earth, if they wish to do so. Christians claim to understand much about the purpose of life. Christians who live by their faith may help the world face the problems of modern life.

As we move toward the end of the twentieth century, Christians and other human beings confront major problems. The peace so stressed in Christ's proclamation is missing in the world. Wars are breaking out; and the possibility of a total war with atomic destruction hangs like a sword over the head of everyone. We are able to destroy human life on earth.

While peace and disarmament seem to be the most urgent needs, another science is taking on enormous importance for all: genetics, the study of human life and its reproduction. Many leaders try to alert people to the temptation to treat life as a mere laboratory object and forget human dignity.

We face an energy crisis. But we do not consider very seriously a new lifestyle which might be humanly richer even though seemingly poorer.

The production of nuclear energy has been initiated before effective safeguards for disposing of harmful wastes have been worked out.

The pressure to obtain oil and minerals has led to threats to the natural environment and to native peoples, as in the tundra of Alaska and jungles of Brazil.

The gap between the rich and poor of the world remains as great as ever. The economies of poorer nations often do not benefit their own citizens but meet the desires of wealthier nations.

To insure their own peace and quiet, people have accepted in silence actual genocide, of the Armenians in the 1920s, the Jews in the 1930s and 1940s, and the Cambodians and Vietnamese in the 1970s.

Applied to the issues of our day, the Christian faith may bring hope to society. What does the faith say about human life? That we are entrusted with the fragile gifts of life and our physical environment. That it is foolish to put complete trust in any human person or idea. That every human being is of eternal value. That the whole human family is one. Christians living out these teachings more fully will help the world through the overwhelming problems that confront the modern world.

59. We leave our story of the Church's history amidst the high peaks of the Andes, looking down and out at Christian people everywhere, all joined in a history— a great adventure—that stretches back to the first Christian Pentecost and forward to a resurrection still wrapped in mystery.

History must end when we reach the present, and so this history ends in a small village in the Andes Mountains of South America. Of course we might have ended it in numberless other places—in great cities or lonely farmsteads, in areas where the color of people's skin is yellow or black or white instead of where it is brown. We might have ended this history in a mighty cathedral or in a humble little chapel, or in a factory, a prison camp, a ship at sea, a skyscraper in New York, a shack in Bombay. We might even have ended within the butter-yellow walls of old Jerusalem where it all began the first Pentecost morning, when the tiny band of Jesus' followers, confused and afraid, experienced the coming of the Holy Spirit in the form of tongues of fire. For the Church still lives in Jerusalem today, still gives its witness, still awaits the return of Jesus.

But to leave our story amidst the high peaks of the Andes has its advantages. From there we can look down, as it were, upon Christian people everywhere and see that despite their faults and failures they continue to find their inspiration in the same gospel the apostles preached and died to defend. Though the Andean villagers are far from well educated as the world judges such things, yet they know that their full humanity is best expressed in Christ, and they try, in their weaknesses as well as in their strengths, to carry on that expression in union with him. In doing so they join themselves to all the Christians who have gone before, to martyrs and missionaries and scholars, to heroes and heroines we have heard about, to others whose heroism is known only to God. For the history of the Christian people is a seamless robe which joins us all in a great adventure, which stretches back to the first Pentecost and forward to a resurrection still wrapped in mystery. Trouble is always with us, and imperfection, and temptation, but we take strength that the same afflictions were with those who went before us. And if they kept faith, so can we.

When Pope John Paul came to Latin America, he said that being Christian meant being a person of one's own land and time and yet also being committed to hopes and values that time cannot affect. So we look from our Andean mountaintop to another mountain town, to Jerusalem, where Jesus said, "Wherever two or three are gathered in my name, there am I in the midst of them."

Outline by Chapter

The Church Today
1920 - 1981

Between Two World Wars (1919-1939)

- 1-2 Europe after World War I
- 3 The Liturgical Movement in the Roman Catholic Church
- 4 Pope Pius XI and the opening of the Catholic Church to modern knowledge
- 5 Catholic and Protestant missionary work
- 6 Missionary activities in Africa
- 7 Muslims in the Middle East; The modernization of Turkey and Iran
- 8 Judaism and the nation of Israel; Anti-Semitism
- 9 The Catholic Church in Mexico; Anti-clericalism and persecution
- 10 The Russian Orthodox Church under Communist rule
- 11-12 Social concerns in the American Catholic Church: The United States Catholic Conference; Dorothy Day and the Catholic Worker; Bishop Bernard Sheil and labor; Catherine de Hueck and Friendship House
- 13 Modern architecture: Skyscrapers; Frank Lloyd Wright; The Bauhaus
- 14 Totalitarian rule in Europe; The Holocaust of European Jews
- 15 The Catholic Church in China and Japan
- 16 The Catholic Church in France: Jacques Maritain; Emmanuel Mounier
- 17 The Catholic Church's agreements with the governments of Italy and Germany
- 18 Protestant theologians: Karl Barth; Rudolf Bultmann; Leonard Ragaz; Paul Tillich; Reinhold Niebuhr
- 19 Christian response to Nazism: The papal encyclical; The Confessing Church of Germany

World War II (1939-1945) and After

- 20 World War II
- 21 Pope Pius XII during the war years
- 22 Christian martyrs under Nazism: Dietrich Bonhoeffer and Maximilian Kolbe
- 23 Existentialism
- 24 The United Nations; The Marshall Plan; Formation of the Communist bloc and the Western bloc
- 25 Gandhi of India
- 26 The World Council of Churches
- 27 European Catholic theologians: de Lubac; Congar; Schillebeeckx
- 28 The worker-priest movement in France; Jacques Loew and the School of Faith
- 29 The Liturgical Movement; Secular Institutes
- 30 The Church in Communist countries; "The Church of Silence"
- 31 Teilhard de Chardin
- 32 Christian involvement in politics in Europe and America
- 33 Pastoral work among immigrants
- 34 History of the Catholic school system in the U.S.
- 35 Independence for Arab and African nations
- 36 The rise of international charitable organizations: Catholic Relief Services; Lutheran World Service; Anglican Consultative Union
- 37-38 Pope John XXIII and Vatican Council II
- 39-40 Vatican II: Openness to the world
- 41 Pope Paul VI's efforts for peace and cooperation among nations

42 The Church in Africa

43 Liberation movements

44 The Church in the Far East

45 Martin Luther King, Jr. and the civil rights movement; Protestant city mission work

46 Latin America: Theology of Liberation; The Medellín Conference

47 Crisis in the Catholic Church after Vatican II

48 Theology in the Roman Catholic Church: Karl Rahner; Hans Urs von Balthasar; Hans Küng

49 The influence of the Russian Orthodox Church in the West after 1917

50 The Russian Orthodox Church in Soviet Russia under Communism

51 Christian life in other Communist nations of Europe

52 "The whole Church is missionary"

53 Charismatic renewal

54-55 Movements of renewal in the Church: Bread for the World; Sword of the Spirit; the Grail; Cursillo; Focolari; Communion and Liberation; Oases; religious retreats

56 Mother Teresa of Calcutta; Jean Vanier and Ark

57 Pope John Paul II

58 Christian responsibility in the twentieth century

59 "History must end when we reach the present"

Chapters 1 through 17 were translated and revised by John Drury, and then further reworked by the editorial staff of Winston Press.

Chapters 46 and 59, by Marvin R. O'Connell

Chapters 37-40 and 47, by James Bitney